D0757613

After the Neocons

AMERICA

AT THE

CROSSROADS

Francis Fukuyama

P
PROFILE BOOKS

First published in Great Britain in 2006 by
PROFILE BOOKS LTD
3A Exmouth House
Pine Street
London EC1R 0JH
www.profilebooks.com

First published in the United States of America in 2006 by
Yale University Press

5 7 9 10 8 6 4

Printed and bound in Great Britain by
William Clowes Ltd, Beccles, Suffolk

A CIP catalogue record for this book is available from the British Library.

ISBN-10 1 86197 922 3
ISBN-13 978 1 86197 922 3

Contents

Preface

The subject of this book is American foreign policy since the al-Qaida attacks of September 11, 2001. This is a personal subject for me. Having long regarded myself as a neoconservative, I thought I shared a common worldview with many other neoconservatives—including friends and acquaintances who served in the administration of George W. Bush. I worked for former Deputy Secretary of Defense Paul D. Wolfowitz on two occasions, first at the U.S. Arms Control and Disarmament Agency and later at the State Department; he was also responsible for recruiting me to come to the Johns Hopkins School of Advanced International Studies while he was dean there. I worked with his mentor Albert Wohlstetter at the latter's consulting firm, Pan Heuristics, and like him was an analyst for several years at the Rand Corporation. I was a student of Allan Bloom, himself a student of Leo Strauss and the author of *The Closing of the American Mind*. I was a classmate of William Kristol in graduate school and wrote frequently for the two magazines founded by his father, Irving Kristol, *The National Interest* and *The Public Interest*, as well as for *Commentary* magazine.

And yet, unlike many other neoconservatives, I was never persuaded of the rationale for the Iraq war. I started out fairly hawkish on Iraq and in 1998 signed a letter sponsored by the Project for the New American Century urging the Clinton Administration to take a harder line against Baghdad after Saddam Hussein blocked the United Nations weapons inspectors. An American invasion of Iraq was not then in the cards, however, and would not be until the events of September 11, 2001. In the year immediately preceding the invasion, I was asked to participate in a study on long-term U.S. strategy toward the war on terrorism. It was at this point that I finally decided the war didn't make sense, and the study gave me an opportunity to think through many of the issues in the present book. I have spent much time since then wondering whether I had somehow changed my views in a way that disqualified me as a neoconservative or whether the neoconservative supporters of the war were misapplying common principles we all still shared.

The disjuncture between what I believed and what other neoconservatives seemed to believe was brought home to me in February 2004 when I attended the annual dinner of the American Enterprise Institute, at which the syndicated columnist Charles

Krauthammer delivered the annual Irving Kristol address entitled "Democratic Realism: An American Foreign Policy for a Unipolar World." This speech, given almost a year after the U.S. invasion of Iraq, treated the war as a virtually unqualified success. I could not understand why everyone around me was applauding the speech enthusiastically, given that the United States had found no weapons of mass destruction in Iraq, was bogged down in a vicious insurgency, and had almost totally isolated itself from the rest of the world by following the kind of unipolar strategy advocated by Krauthammer. The following day I ran into the then-editor of *The National Interest*, John O'Sullivan, and told him that I wanted to write up a critique. He agreed on the spot, and the result was an article entitled "The Neo-Conservative Moment," which appeared in the summer of 2004.

I have concluded that neoconservatism, as both a political symbol and a body of thought, has evolved into something that I can no longer support. As I will try to demonstrate in this book, neoconservatism was based on a set of coherent principles that during the Cold War yielded by and large sensible policies both at home and abroad. The principles, however, could be interpreted in a variety of ways, and during the 1990s they were used to justify an American foreign policy that overemphasized the use of force and led logically to the Iraq war. Neoconservatism has now become irreversibly identified with the policies of the administration of George W. Bush in its first term, and any effort to reclaim the label at this point is likely to be futile. It is much more important to redefine American foreign policy in a way that moves beyond the Bush administration's legacy and that of its neoconservative supporters.

This book is an attempt to elucidate the neoconservative legacy, explain where in my view the Bush administration has gone wrong, and outline an alternative way for the United States to relate to the rest of the world. This has also motivated my effort to start a new journal devoted to the question of America's role in the world, *The American Interest* (www.the-american-interest.com). The position I want to stake out is not captured by any existing schools within the U.S. foreign policy debate, but it is one that I think would win support from a fairly broad spectrum of Americans. I have labeled it "realistic Wilsonianism," which is an admittedly awkward locution since both realism and Woodrow Wilson's legacy are heavily loaded concepts. If anyone can think of a better label, he or she is welcome to contact me with suggestions.

Careful readers of my original critique of Krauthammer will note that the present volume is missing a line of argument present in the earlier piece, concerning the way that certain neoconservatives had internalized a hard-line Israeli strategic doctrine and applied it, inappropriately in my view, to the situation of the United States after September 11. This is particularly true of Charles Krauthammer, and our subsequent exchanges convince me that I was right about this. His apocalyptic view of the threat from the Muslim world is wrong in my view, for reasons I lay out in Chapter 3. But this particular point of view, while true of certain individuals, cannot be attributed to neoconservatives more broadly, nor can it be laid at the doorstep of the Bush administration. There are a number of things I wish the administration had done differently with regard to the Israeli-Palestinian conflict. However, I do not think the circumstances for making a big push toward a final settlement of the Israeli-Palestinian conflict were propitious during the administration's first four years. As long as Yasser Arafat was alive, there was little chance of political reform in the Palestinian Authority or of a Palestinian interlocutor that could reach and enforce a peace agreement with Israel. The real test for the Bush administration on this and other neoconservative issues will come in its second term, after the pullout from Gaza.

The materials in this book were initially presented as the Castle Lectures, which I delivered at Yale University on April 11, 12, and 18, 2005. I would like to thank the Program in Ethics, Politics, and Economics, which hosted the lecture series, and its director, Seyla Benhabib, who initially invited me to deliver it. I am also grateful to John K. Castle, who funded the series to honor his ancestor, the Reverend James Pierpoint.

A great many people provided comments on the manuscript or else responded when it was presented publicly, including Robert Boynton, Mark Cordover, Charles Davidson, Hillel Fradkin, Adam Garfinkle, John Ikenberry, Roger Leeds, Mark Lilla, Mike Mandelbaum, Trita Parsi, Marc Plattner, Jeremy Rabkin, Stephen Sestanovich, Abram Shulsky, Tom White, and Adam

Wolfson. I would also like to thank John Lewis Gaddis and Steven Smith, who served as reviewers for Yale University Press. John Kulka, senior editor at the press, provided helpful guidance as the manuscript evolved. I have greatly benefited from numerous conversations with Stephen Hosmer, one of the wisest people I know on the subject of American policy in developing countries. A number of other people contributed ideas and discussions that were eventually incorporated into the book (whether they know it or not), including Peter Berkowitz, Zbigniew Brzezinski, Kurt Campbell, Eliot Cohen, Ivo Daalder, Mike Desch, Barbara Haig, Leon Kass, Tom Keaney, Tod Lindberg, Rob Litwak, John Mearsheimer, Nathan Tarcov, and Ken Weinstein. My wife, Laura Holmgren, was a skeptic about the war from the beginning, and I profited from many discussions with her about it. My assistant Cynthia Doroghazi helped in many different phases of this project. Carlos Hamann, Ina Hoxha, and Krystof Monasterski served as research assistants. I am, finally, grateful to my team of resourceful literary agents at International Creative Management, Esther Newberg, Christine Bauch, Betsy Robbins, Margaret Halton, and Liz Iveson, for helping make the present volume possible.

1 *Principles and Prudence*

During the first term of George W. Bush's presidency, the United States was attacked on its own soil by the radical Islamist group al-Qaida, in the single most destructive terrorist act in history. The Bush administration responded to this unprecedented event with dramatic and sweeping new policies. First, it created an entirely new federal agency, the Department of Homeland Security, and pushed through Congress the Patriot Act, designed to give domestic law enforcement greater powers to act against would-be terrorists. Second, it invaded Afghanistan, a land-locked country on the other side of the world, and deposed the Taliban regime there that had sheltered al-Qaida. Third, it announced a new strategic doctrine of preemptive action—actually, a doctrine of preventive war—that would take the fight to the enemy, rather than relying on deterrence and containment that were the staples of

Cold War policy. And fourth, it invaded and deposed the regime of Saddam Hussein on the grounds that he had or was planning to acquire weapons of mass destruction (WMD).

The first two of these initiatives were inevitable responses to the September 11 attacks, urged by members of both political parties and supported by an overwhelming majority of the American people. While some have criticized aspects of the Patriot Act as impinging excessively on individual liberties, it is hard to imagine that the nation would have continued in its lackadaisical approach to homeland security after the World Trade Center and Pentagon attacks.

The second two initiatives, however—announcement of a broad preemptive doctrine and the invasion of Iraq—were not obvious responses to September 11. Both policies could be justified on a number of grounds. What made them especially controversial, however, was the almost obsessive emphasis that the Bush administration placed on regime change in Iraq and the implicit assertion of American exceptionalism that gave Washington not just the right but the duty to take care of this problem. Various administration officials, beginning with the president himself, made clear that the United States would proceed against Saddam regardless of the views of its allies. This decision had evidently already been made by the summer of 2002, before the reentry of U.N. weapons inspectors into Iraq or formal Security Council debate.[1] Although the United States made clear that it would be happy to receive support from the Security Council, it felt in no way constrained by what its allies or the broader international community thought. The Bush administration expected a short war and a quick and relatively painless transition to a post-Saddam Iraq. It gave little thought to the requirements for post-conflict reconstruction and was surprised to find the United States fighting a prolonged insurgency.

Neoconservative intellectuals, in their years out of power before the 2000 election, had proposed a foreign policy agenda involving concepts like regime change, benevolent hegemony, unipolarity, preemption, and American exceptionalism that came to be hallmarks of the Bush administration's foreign policy. Many neoconservatives were strong public advocates of the war and defended the shift in focus from al-Qaida to Iraq. Moreover, the Bush administration has left a relatively rich doctrinal record of its own thinking on grand strategy in the form of speeches and policy statements such as the president's state of the union and inaugural addresses, his West Point and American Enterprise Institute speeches in June 2002 and February 2003, and the *National Security Strategy of the United States*, published in September 2002. Collectively, these have been informally labeled the Bush Doctrine. These official pronouncements are consistent with what neoconservatives outside the administration were arguing; indeed, in the case of Bush's second inaugural, some outsiders provided ideas directly. Given this record, it is not surprising that many observers saw the Bush administration as being decisively shaped by neoconservatives.

But while there is reason for associating neoconservatism with Bush's first-term policies, a central theme of this book will be that the connection is often overstated and glosses over a much more complex reality. Until memoirs are written and future historians do their work, we will not know the degree to which key figures in the administration were driven by larger ideas, as opposed to muddling through in response to fast-changing events. The administration principals most in favor of the war—Defense Secretary Donald Rumsfeld and Vice President Dick Cheney—were not known as neoconservatives before their tenures, and we do not at this point know the origins of their views.

More important, even if ideas were drivers of policy, the ideas held by neoconservatives were themselves complex and subject to differing interpretations. The administration's foreign policy in particular did not flow ineluctably from the views of earlier generations of people who considered themselves neoconservatives. The neoconservative legacy is complex and diverse, tracing its roots back to the early 1940s. It has generated a coherent body of ideas that informed a wide range of domestic and foreign policy choices.

Four common principles or threads ran through much of this thought up through the end of the Cold War: a concern with democracy, human rights, and more generally the internal politics of states; a belief that U.S. power can be used for moral purposes; a skepticism about the ability of international law and institutions to solve serious security problems; and finally, a view that

4

ambitious social engineering often leads to unexpected consequences and often undermines its own ends.

When they are stated in this abstract fashion, most Americans
would find little to object to in these principles: Henry Kissinger
and his realist disciples would not deny that democracy is important, while supporters of the United Nations will concede that
organization's limitations and failings. One is thus inclined to
conclude that the Bush administration's mistakes were simply errors of prudential judgment or policy implementation, rather
than reflections of underlying principles.

The problem is not that simple, however, because the abstract
ideas were interpreted in certain characteristic ways that might
better be described as mindsets or worldviews rather than principled positions. The prudential choices that flowed from these
mindsets were biased in certain consistent directions that made
them, when they proved to be wrong, something more than individual errors of judgment. There were three main areas of what
we might call biased judgment that led to mistakes on the part of
the Bush administration in its stewardship of U.S. foreign policy
in its first term.

The first was threat assessment. The administration overestimated, or perhaps more accurately mischaracterized, the
threat facing the United States from radical Islamism. Although
the new and ominous possibility of undeterrable terrorists armed
with weapons of mass destruction did indeed present itself, the
administration wrongly conflated this with the threat presented

by Iraq and with the rogue state/proliferation problem more generally. The misjudgment was based in part on the massive failure of the U.S. intelligence community to correctly assess the state of Iraq's WMD programs before the war. But the intelligence community never took nearly as alarmist a view of the terrorist/WMD threat as did the administration itself. Overestimation of this threat then justified the elevation of preventive war as the centerpiece of a new security strategy. The administration argued that September 11 had made preventive war necessary as a means of taking the fight to the enemy, but that argument made sense only if the real enemy had been correctly identified.

In addition, the Bush administration failed to anticipate the virulently negative global reaction to its exercise of "benevolent hegemony." The administration came into office with a strong ideological bias against the United Nations and other international organizations such as the International Criminal Court. Officials failed to recognize that they were pushing against a strong undertow of anti-Americanism that would be greatly exacerbated by their seemingly contemptuous brush-off of most forms of international cooperation. The emergence of a unipolar post–Cold War world had made the extent of American hegemony, as it turned out, a source of anxiety even to America's closest allies.

Finally, the Bush administration failed to anticipate the requirements for pacifying and reconstructing Iraq, and was wildly overoptimistic in its assessment of the ease with which large-scale social engineering could be accomplished not just in Iraq but in the Middle East as a whole. This could not have been a failure of underlying principle, since a consistent neoconservative theme, as noted above, had been skepticism about the prospects for social engineering. Rather, proponents of the war seem to have forgotten their own principles in the heat of their advocacy of the war.

Whatever its complex roots, neoconservatism has now become inevitably linked to concepts like preemption, regime change, unilateralism, and benevolent hegemony as put into practice by the Bush administration. Rather than attempting the feckless task of reclaiming the meaning of the term, it seems to me better to abandon the label and articulate an altogether distinct foreign policy position.

Neoconservatism is one of four different approaches to American foreign policy today. There are, in addition to neoconservatives, "realists" in the tradition of Henry Kissinger, who respect power and tend to downplay the internal nature of other regimes and human rights concerns; there are liberal internationalists who hope to transcend power politics altogether and move to an international order based on law and institutions; and there are what Walter Russell Mead labels "Jacksonian" American nationalists, who tend to take a narrow, security-related view of American national interests, distrust multilateralism, and in their more extreme manifestations tend toward nativism and isolationism.[2] The Iraq war was promoted by an alliance of neoconservatives and Jacksonian nationalists, who for different reasons accepted the logic of regime change in Baghdad. They sidelined the realists in the Republican Party like Brent Scowcroft and James Baker, who had served in George Herbert Walker Bush's administration and were skeptical about the rationale for the war.

As Operation Iraqi Freedom degenerated from a triumphant liberation to a grinding occupation and guerrilla war, the neoconservatives found themselves on the defensive, and the realists started to gain ground. The neoconservatives regained their position after the January 30, 2005, Iraqi elections but lost it again as the insurgency continued. There will certainly be further ups and downs as the consequences of the war play themselves out that will, once again, change the relative authority of one faction over the other. The problem is that none of these positions—neoconservative, realist, Jacksonian nationalist, or liberal internationalist—properly defines the approach to the world that the United States needs to follow in the aftermath of September 11 and the invasion of Iraq. The realist and neoconservative positions in particular were defined partly in opposition to each other during the Cold War, and both are inadequate to the world that is emerging in the twenty-first century. That world is characterized by American hegemony and a global anti-American backlash, complete with inchoate forms of "soft" balancing; a shift in the locus of action away from nation-states toward non-state actors and other transnational forces; an accompanying disintegration of sovereignty both as a normative principle and as an empirical reality; and the emergence of a band of weak and failed states that are the source of most global problems.

In light of this emerging external environment, the United States needs to define an approach to foreign policy that is not captured by any of these existing positions. This approach begins from certain neoconservative premises: first, that U.S. policy and the international community more broadly need to concern themselves with what goes on *inside* other countries, not just their external behavior, as realists would have it; and second, that power—specifically American power—is often necessary to bring about moral purposes. It also draws on a neoconservative principle that neoconservatives seemed to have forgotten in the lead-up to the Iraq war: namely, that ambitious social engineering is very difficult and ought always to be approached with care and humility. What we need, in other words, is a more realistic Wilsonianism that better matches means to ends in dealing with other societies.

Realistic Wilsonianism differs from classical realism by taking seriously as an object of U.S. foreign policy what goes on inside states. To say that nation-building or democracy promotion is hard is not to say that it is impossible or that it should be scrupulously avoided. Indeed, weak or failed states are one of the biggest sources of global disorder today, and it is simply impossible, for reasons relating both to security and to morality, for the world's sole superpower to walk away from them. Neither realists nor neoconservatives have paid sufficient attention to the problem of development over the years, nor have they focused on parts of the world like Africa or Latin America where development is most problematic (except, of course, when countries in these regions became security threats).

Realistic Wilsonianism differs from neoconservatism (and Jacksonian nationalism) insofar as it takes international institutions seriously. We do not want to replace national sovereignty with unaccountable international organizations; the United Nations is not now nor will it ever become an effective, legitimate seat of global governance. On the other hand, we do not now have an adequate set of horizontal mechanisms of accountability between the vertical stovepipes we label states—adequate, that is, to match the intense economic and social interpenetration that we characterize today as globalization. The state retains a critical function that cannot be replaced by any transnational actor: it remains the only source of power that can enforce a rule of law. But for that power to be effective, it must be seen as legitimate; and durable legitimacy requires a much higher degree of institutionalization *across* nations than exists currently. A multi-institutional world that will meet these needs is gradually coming into being, but we are not there yet, and none of the existing schools of foreign policy provides adequate guidance to get us there.

This book suggests a different way for America to relate to the world, one that is neither neoconservative nor realist, Jacksonian nor liberal internationalist. It attempts to define a more realistic way for the United States to promote political and economic development other than through preemptive war, and opens up an agenda of multiple multilateralisms appropriate to the real, existing world of globalization.

2 The Neoconservative Legacy

In the period leading up to and following the Iraq war, an enormous amount of ink was spilled on the subject of neoconservatives and their alleged capture of the Bush administration. The story is endlessly fascinating because it appears to unlock a conspiratorial key to the administration's behavior. Elizabeth Drew explained in the *New York Review of Books* that "the neoconservatives . . . are largely responsible for getting us into the war against Iraq." This was echoed during the 2004 campaign by Democratic presidential candidate Howard Dean, who charged that the Bush administration had been captured by "neoconservatives." Many commentators pointed to the fact that several prominent proponents of the Iraq war, like Paul Wolfowitz, Douglas Feith, and Richard Perle, were Jewish, and argued that the Iraq policy was ultimately designed to make the Middle East safe for Israel. A separate line of argument blamed the Iraq war on the Straussian wing of the neoconservative movement, charging that Leo Strauss was "a champion of the 'noble lie'—the idea that it is practically a duty to lie to the masses because only a small elite is intellectually fit to know the truth."[1]

Much of this literature is factually wrong, animated by ill will, and a deliberate distortion of the record of both the Bush administration and its supporters. To listen to many of these accounts, one would think that neoconservatism was an alien spore that drifted in from outer space and infected the American body politic. It is perhaps not surprising that some neoconservatives have charged in return that, in the mouths of their critics, *neoconservative* is a code word for *Jewish*, since the kind of takeover of the American body politic alleged is all too similar to the kinds of conspiracies laid at the feet of Jews in the history of anti-Semitism. The ferocious attack on neoconservatism in the wake of the Iraq war has led other neoconservatives to deny that neoconservatism even exists, or that it had any particular relationship to the policies followed by the Bush administration.[2]

The fact of the matter is that the key principles of neoconservatism as they developed from the mid-twentieth century to the present are deeply rooted in a variety of American traditions. Neoconservatism is a coherent set of ideas, arguments, and conclusions from experience that should be judged on its own merits, not on the basis of the ethnic or religious identity of those who espouse those ideas. Nor does it make sense to deny that such a movement exists since two of the godfathers of neoconservatism, Irving Kristol and Norman Podhoretz, wrote essays well before the Iraq war on what neoconservatism was and were happy to explore areas of agreement and disagreement among the various people who identified themselves as neoconservatives.[3]

Those who argue that neoconservatism does not exist point to the fact that there is no established neoconservative "doctrine," as was the case with, for example, Marxism-Leninism, and note the disagreements and contradictions that exist among self-styled neoconservatives. This is all true, but the fact that neoconservatism is not monolithic does not imply that it does not rest on a core of coherent ideas. Rather, it is a confluence of intellectual streams that have resulted in areas of ambiguity or disagreement among neoconservatives.

The Roots of Neoconservatism

Several general accounts of neoconservatism have been written thus far that provide insight into the intellectual origins of the movement. As noted earlier, Kristol and Podhoretz have written their own authoritative accounts of how they came to become neoconservatives. Probably the most balanced history by a non-neoconservative is that of two French journalists, Alain Frachon and Daniel Vernet, in a work entitled *L'Amérique messianique* (2004). In English, James Mann provides personal background on Deputy Defense Secretary Paul Wolfowitz in his *Rise of the Vulcans* (2004). Murray Friedman has written a detailed history of the specifically Jewish intellectual roots of neoconservative thought, and there are of course a legion of inaccurate, hostile, and highly distorted critiques.[4]

The roots of neoconservatism lie in a remarkable group of largely Jewish intellectuals who attended City College of New York (CCNY) in the mid- to late 1930s and early 1940s, a group that included Irving Kristol, Daniel Bell, Irving Howe, Seymour Martin Lipset, Philip Selznick, Nathan Glazer, and, a bit later, Daniel Patrick Moynihan. The story of this group has been told in a number of places, most notably in a Public Broadcasting documentary and in a related book by Joseph Dorman called *Arguing the World* (2001).[5] All these figures came from working-class, immigrant backgrounds and attended CCNY because elite institutions like Columbia and Harvard were largely closed to them. That period, like today, was one of intense crisis in world politics, and the CCNY group was totally politicized and committed to left-wing politics. The story of Alcove 1 in the CCNY cafeteria, which was Trotskyite, and Alcove 2, which was Stalinist, and Irving Kristol's initial flirtation with the former, is by now well known.

Yet the most important inheritance from the CCNY group was an intense *anticommunism* and an almost equal distaste for liberals who sympathized with communism and could not see the evil it represented. Understanding the genesis of this liberal an-

ticommunism is critical to understanding the origins of neoconservatism and the opposition to utopian social engineering that
is the most enduring thread running through the movement.

It is not an accident that many of the CCNY group started out
as Trotskyites. Trotsky was, of course, himself a communist, but
in this period of popular front followed by the Hitler-Stalin pact,
followed by the return to popular front after the German invasion of the Soviet Union, the Trotskyites understood better than
most people the utter cynicism and brutality of the Stalinist
regime. That brutality led Stalin to have Trotsky murdered in
Mexico City in 1940.

The anticommunism of the disillusioned Left is rather different from the anticommunism of the traditional American Right.
The latter opposed communism because it was atheistic, linked
to a hostile foreign power, and anti–free market. The anticom-
munist Left, by contrast, sympathized with the social and economic aims of communism, but in the course of the 1930s and
1940s came to realize that "real existing socialism" had become a
monstrosity of unintended consequences that completely undermined the idealistic goals it espoused. The danger of good intentions carried to extremes was a theme that would underlie the life
work of many members of this group over the next generation.

While virtually all the CCNY group had ceased being Marxist
by the time of World War II, the timing and the distance of their
eventual shift to the right varied: Irving Kristol moved the far-
thest, Irving Howe the least, and Bell, Glazer, Lipset, and Moy-

nihan ended up somewhere in between. The shift right was almost inevitable, not just because of the revelations about the nature of Stalinist terror that were slowly leaking out of the Soviet Union, but also because the capitalist United States intervened against Nazi Germany and played a key role in its defeat and in that of Japan. It was the exercise of seemingly unlimited American power, then, that brought about what all regarded as an extremely moral conclusion to the Second World War.

The hothouse intellectual life of New York in the late 1940s and early 1950s centered around magazines like *Partisan Review* and *Commentary*, and the debate was set against the backdrop of a growing Cold War and McCarthyism, leading over time to further defections from the Left that swelled the ranks of the neo-conservatives. Norman Podhoretz has documented his own journey to the right extensively, and under his editorship *Commentary* moved right as well, to become the leading journal for what became neoconservative thought.[6]

THE PUBLIC INTEREST

There is considerable continuity between the anticommunism of the CCNY group and the second important stream of neoconservative thinking that grew out of the journal *The Public Interest*, founded in 1965 by Irving Kristol and Daniel Bell (who was soon replaced as co-editor by Nathan Glazer). American politics had shifted dramatically by the late 1960s: as a result of the civil rights movement and the Vietnam War, the old communist and fellow-traveling Left of the 1930s had been replaced, temporarily at least, by the New Left of Tom Hayden and the Students for a Democratic Society. This was also the period of the revival of large-scale social engineering on the part of the U.S. government, in the form of Lyndon Johnson's War on Poverty and Great Society programs. Figures like Bell, Glazer, and Lipset were by now all ensconced in universities and found themselves in opposition to a new generation of student radicals who, in addition to supporting a progressive social agenda with which their professors were vaguely sympathetic, attacked the university itself as a handmaiden of American capitalism and imperialism.

The first formative battle that shaped neoconservatism was the fight with the Stalinists in the thirties and forties; the second was the one with the New Left and the Counterculture it spawned in the 1960s. The second battle had both foreign and domestic policy dimensions. Opposition to the Vietnam War bred a generation of American leftists who were sympathetic to communist or Marxist regimes in Havana, Hanoi, Beijing, and Managua; it also led to an ambitious domestic agenda that sought to emulate European welfare states and address many of the underlying causes of social inequality.

The Public Interest was founded by Kristol and Bell precisely to cast a critical, though often sympathetic, eye on the domestic part of the agenda. This journal became home to a generation of academics, social scientists, and think-tank intellectuals including Glazer, Moynihan, James Q. Wilson, Glenn Loury, Charles

Murray, and Stephan and Abigail Thernstrom. These writers put forward a critique of the Great Society that laid the intellectual groundwork for the subsequent shift to the right in social policy of the 1980s and 1990s.

If there is a single overarching theme to the domestic social policy critiques carried out by those who wrote for *The Public Interest*, it is the limits of social engineering. Ambitious efforts to seek social justice, these writers argued, often left societies worse off than before because they either required massive state intervention that disrupted organic social relations (for example, forced busing) or else produced unanticipated consequences (such as an increase in single-parent families as a result of welfare). There was thus a direct link between the critique of American public policy and the earlier anticommunism of the CCNY group: both American liberals and Soviet communists sought worthy ends but undermined themselves by failing to recognize the limits of political voluntarism.

Examples of this focus abound. Nathan Glazer wrote about the negative consequences of affirmative action in terms of the way it stigmatized its purported beneficiaries and set up perverse incentives for social advancement. James Q. Wilson, in his extensive writings on crime, argued that it was foolish to believe that social policy could get at alleged root causes of crime like poverty and racism, and that sensible crime-fighting policies had to deal with mitigating short-term symptoms. His famous "Broken Windows" article (written with George Kelling) argued that police departments ought to focus on smaller issues of social order as well as major crimes; it had the remarkable effect of persuading New York City to clean the graffiti off of its subway cars.[7]

Daniel Patrick Moynihan was perhaps most famous for his 1965 study *The Negro Family*, which argued that black poverty had complex origins in culture and family structure and could not be solved through incentives that failed to take account of social habit. The Moynihan report was highly controversial when first issued and led to a thunderous and consequential debate on the "culture of poverty." Moynihan's critique was extended by Charles Murray, who pointed to the unanticipated consequences of welfare programs like Aid to Families with Dependent Children (AFDC), which encouraged out-of-wedlock births and contributed to the culture of poverty.[8] This critique of AFDC led ultimately to its abolition under the Personal Responsibility and Work Opportunity Reconciliation Act of 1996, initiated by the Republican Congress and signed by President Bill Clinton.

The Public Interest dealt exclusively with domestic policy. Irving Kristol went on to found a companion journal on foreign policy, *The National Interest*, which, under the stewardship of its founding editor, Owen Harries, hosted a great diversity of views, broadly right of center, on U.S. foreign policy. The critique of domestic policy begun by *The Public Interest* would ultimately have implications for U.S. foreign policy, but the connection was not a direct one and was never made by many neoconservatives.

The more proximate origins of neoconservative foreign policy lie elsewhere.

More nonsense has been written about Leo Strauss and the Iraq war than on virtually any other subject. Mark Lilla published a long and informative account of who Strauss was and has ably defended Strauss from careless charges flung around by Anne Norton, Shadia Drury, Lyndon LaRouche, and others to the effect that he propounded a secret antidemocratic teaching or promoted lying on the part of public officials.[9] Among the reasons why it is silly to think that Strauss had an impact on the Bush administration's foreign policy is the fact that there were no Straussians serving in the administration in the lead-up to the Iraq war. If you were to ask Dick Cheney, Donald Rumsfeld, or President Bush himself to explain who Leo Strauss was, you would probably draw blank stares.

The idea of Straussian influence gained currency only because Paul Wolfowitz, the deputy secretary of defense, studied briefly with Strauss and with Allan Bloom, who was himself a student of Strauss. But Wolfowitz never regarded himself as a Strauss protégé, and his foreign policy views were much more heavily influenced by other teachers, in particular Albert Wohlstetter.

Leo Strauss was a German Jewish political theorist who studied under Ernst Cassirer and who, fleeing the Nazis, emigrated to the United States in the 1930s and taught mostly at the University of Chicago until shortly before his death in 1973. Much of his work can be seen as a response to Nietzsche and Heidegger, who had undermined the rationalist tradition of Western philosophy from within and left modernity without a deep philosophical grounding for its own beliefs and institutions. In addition, he wrestled throughout his life with the "theological-political problem" that divine revelation and suprapolitical claims about the nature of the good life could not be banished from political philosophy as easily as the European Enlightenment had thought.

Strauss's response to contemporary relativism was to seek to recover premodern philosophical modes of thought through the careful reading of earlier thinkers, and in particular to engender appreciation for the effort of classical political philosophers to seek a rational account of nature and understand its relation to political life. The bulk of his writings are therefore not doctrinal tracts but rather long and dense interpretive essays on Plato, Thucydides, Alfarabi, Maimonides, Machiavelli, Hobbes, and other philosophers. Strauss did not produce doctrine in the sense that Marx and Lenin did, and it is extraordinarily hard to extract from his writings anything that looks like public policy analysis.

Strauss did, of course, have political opinions: he strongly preferred liberal democracy to communism or fascism; he greatly admired Winston Churchill for standing up to these totalitarian ideologies; and he worried that the philosophical crisis of modernity might undermine the West's self-confidence. But what he imparted to his students was not a set of public policy directives but rather a desire to take seriously and understand the Western philosophical tradition.

Mark Lilla argues that whereas Strauss himself was deeply philosophical and took pains to prevent the politicization of his ideas, his second-, third-, and nth-generation students began to take his teachings not as an invitation to open-ended inquiry but as a catechism. According to Lilla, they began to politicize Strauss's ideas and associate them with particular contemporary public policy prescriptions. Two of Strauss's students played key roles in this transition, Harry Jaffa of Claremont and the late Allan Bloom, who fostered what Lilla identifies as the "Sousa" and "Wagnerian" wings of Straussianism, respectively. Jaffa, drawing heavily on Jefferson's reference to natural right in the Declaration of Independence, associated the American regime with the classical tradition of natural law. His students tended to see the United States as the apotheosis of the philosophical tradition stemming from Plato and Aristotle, thus merging Strauss's philosophical concerns with American nationalism.[10]

Bloom, on the other hand, tended to be much more pessimistic about the disintegrative consequences of the "crisis of modernity," which he saw being played out in American politics and social life. His 1987 best seller, *The Closing of the American Mind*, directly and brilliantly connected Heidegger's *Rectoratsrede* with the contemporary crisis of the American university, as well as with sex, drugs, music, and other trends in popular culture.[11] This book touched a raw nerve and identified a real problem. Cultural relativism—the belief that reason was incapable of rising above the cultural horizons that people inherited—had in fact become ensconced in contemporary intellectual life. It was legitimated at a high level by serious thinkers like Nietzsche and Heidegger, transmitted through intellectual fads like postmodernism and deconstructionism, and translated into practice by cultural anthropology and other parts of the contemporary academy. These ideas found fertile ground in the egalitarianism of American political culture, whose participants objected to having their "lifestyle" choices criticized. And there is no question that this kind of relativism was one of the preconditions for the failure of so many academics and university administrators to defend their own ideals in the face of the assault on the university that occurred during the 1960s. Bloom was interested in philosophical ideas and liberal education rather than policy; he denied overtly that he was a conservative of any sort.

As noted earlier, the progenitors of the neoconservative movement like Daniel Bell and Nathan Glazer also found themselves on the conservative side of the fight with the New Left and student radicalism during the 1960s. What Bloom later provided that they could not articulate at the time was a much deeper understanding of the sources of weakness of contemporary liberal democracy. The kinds of philosophical thinkers, such as Isaiah Berlin and Karl Popper, who were often invoked to support and defend a liberal, pluralistic society, were not anywhere near Strauss's level of philosophical sophistication. So it is perhaps not a surprise that those influenced by Strauss, Jaffa, or Bloom should start migrating to neoconservative circles during the 1980s.

There is one particular idea associated with Strauss and Straussians that does have relevance to the foreign policy of the Bush administration: the idea of "regime." The centrality of the regime to political life comes not from Strauss but ultimately from a reading of Plato and Aristotle, both of whom talk extensively about the nature of aristocratic, monarchic, and democratic regimes and their effects on the character of the people who live under them. Both Plato and Aristotle understand a regime not in the modern way, as a set of visible formal institutions, but rather as a way of life in which formal political institutions and informal habits constantly shape one another. A democratic regime produces a certain kind of citizen: hence Socrates' famous description, in book 8 of the *Republic*, of democratic man: "Then, I said, he also lives along day by day, gratifying the desire that occurs to him, at one time drinking and listening to the flute, at another downing water and reducing; now practicing gymnastic, and again idling and neglecting everything; and sometimes spending his time as though he were occupied with philosophy. Often he engages in politics and, jumping up, says and does whatever chances to come to him; and if he ever admires any soldiers, he turns in that direction; and if it's money-makers, in that one. And there is neither order nor necessity in his life, but calling this life sweet, free, and blessed he follows it throughout."[12]

Among modern political thinkers, Alexis de Tocqueville came

closest to capturing this ancient sense of regime. When he described the American regime in *Democracy in America*, he began with an analysis of its formal institutions: the Constitution, federalism, and the nature of laws in the different American states. But what was particularly insightful about Tocqueville's book were his observations about the habits, customs, and social mores of the American people: their proclivity for voluntary association, the nature of their religiosity, their moralism, their inordinate pride in their own democratic institutions. Tocqueville, who came from an aristocratic French family, had a somewhat less jaundiced view than Socrates of the effects of democracy on human character, but, like Socrates, he believed that a regime's effects on character are central to an understanding of its nature. Tocqueville argued that the American regime was founded on an idea of equality that defined its political institutions but also permeated the behavior and beliefs of its citizens. Those informal habits—the sociological and anthropological layers of political life—in turn sustained and made possible the formal political institutions. Thus regime, understood in this broader sense, was key to an understanding of political life.

A theme that appears in Strauss's writings and those of many of his students is the role of politics in the shaping of regimes. In *Natural Right and History* (1953), Strauss criticizes the British Whig thinker Edmund Burke for arguing that good political orders tended to be based on the historical accretions of traditions, customs, values, and mores. Strauss, like Plato and Aristotle, believed that a discussion of the ends of common life could not be banished from political life altogether, as the modern liberal project tried to do. Moreover (to put it in non-Straussian terminology), formal political institutions played a crucial role in shaping informal cultural norms and habits. There is a great deal of discussion among Straussians about regime "founding," though almost always in the context of historical cases like Solon, Lycurgus, or the American founding fathers. With regard to the latter, virtually all Straussians, whether Sousa or Wagnerian, believe that the American character was decisively shaped by the political institutions that Americans chose for themselves in the period between 1776 and 1789. Those institutions, in turn, were not simply ratifications of a long-term and bottom-up Burkean common-law process. They were at times informed by explicit rational debate, such as that contained in the Federalist Papers, which occasionally rose to the level of genuine philosophical reflection.[13] This view of the centrality of politics, incidentally, was shared by Tocqueville, who believed that the idea of political equality embedded in American institutions explained the habits and mores that Americans later came to exhibit.

Thus Strauss was neither antipolitical nor antistatist; he, like Aristotle, believed that humans were political by nature and reached their full flourishing only by participating in the life of the city. This is why the Straussian wing of the neoconservative movement always had a problem with libertarian conservatives. Libertarians understand freedom only negatively, as freedom from government power. In the words of Adam Wolfson, "Libertarians rise to the defense of every conceivable freedom but that of self-government. . . . To the neoconservative, the true road to serfdom lies in the efforts of libertarian and left-wing elites to mandate an anti-democratic social policy all in the name of liberty. But it is a narrow, privatized liberty that is secured. An active and lively interest in public affairs is discouraged as a result. Everything is permitted except a say in the shaping of the public ethos."[14] Thus, while Straussians and neoconservatives more broadly were tactically allied with traditional conservatives and libertarians on issues like welfare reform, they understood the problem very differently. They focused on the corroding effects of welfare on the character of the poor; they did not oppose as a matter of principle state intervention as such.

The Bush administration has put "regime change" front and center in its foreign policy and has reached out with military force and deposed regimes in Afghanistan and Iraq. Does this kind of policy flow from the understanding of the centrality of regime as understood by Strauss and his followers? It partly does and partly does not, in a way that illustrates the extreme difficulty of translating philosophical ideas into actual policies.

The correct part of the implication is that certain political problems can be solved only through regime change. That is, regimes constitute and reflect broad ways of life; though Socrates does not talk about foreign policy, it is hard to imagine that for him the nature of the regime would not affect the external behavior of a society. This idea is implicit in contemporary international relations theories about "democratic peace": nation-states are not black boxes or billiard balls that indifferently compete for power, as realists would have it; foreign policy reflects the values of their underlying societies. Regimes that treat their own citizens unjustly are likely to do the same to foreigners. Thus efforts to change the behavior of tyrannical or totalitarian regimes through external rewards or punishments will always be less effective than changing the underlying nature of the regime. Poland, Hungary, and Czechoslovakia were communist regimes and members of the Warsaw Pact before 1989; the threat they represented to Western Europe was mitigated ultimately not through arms control deals like the Conventional Forces in Europe negotiations but through their transformation into liberal democracies.

So far, so good: regime change in Afghanistan and Iraq are ultimately the best guarantees that they will not threaten the United States or their neighbors as the Taliban and Saddam Hussein did. Strauss's understanding of the centrality of politics would also have suggested that successful regime change would in the long run have a positive effect on the habits and mores of the society. Saddam Hussein's tyranny bred passivity and fatalism—not to mention vices of cruelty and violence—whereas a democratic Iraq would presumably foster greater individual self-reliance.

But a correct understanding of the Straussian interpretation of regime would also have raised red flags over the American effort to bring about regime change. Regimes by this understanding are not just formal institutions and authority structures; they shape and are shaped by the societies underlying them. The unwritten rules by which people operate, based on religion, kinship, and shared historical experience, are also part of the regime. While classical political philosophy suggests that the founding of new regimes can lead to new ways of life, it does not argue that they are particularly easy to found. Plato in particular emphasizes the need for something like a civic religion to persuade people that their here-and-now political order is grounded in the larger order of the cosmos. This is suggested both by Socrates' elaboration of the myth of Er in book 10 of the *Republic* and by the lengthy discussion of religion in the *Laws*. If there is any central theme to Strauss's skepticism about the modern Enlightenment project, it is the idea that reason alone is sufficient to establish a durable political order or that the nonrational claims of revelation can be banished from politics.

Founding a new political order is, therefore, a difficult business, and doubly so for those who are not immersed in the habits, mores, and traditions of the people for whom they are legislating. Historically, few administrators of the American overseas empire—with the possible exception of Douglas MacArthur—have shown great aptitude for this kind of work.[15] They have tended to bring their American experience to foreign lands, rather than seeing institutions emerging out of the habits and experience of local peoples. There is no Straussian belief in the universality of the American experience; neither Strauss nor any of the ancient political philosophers believed that democracy was the default regime to which societies would revert once dictatorship was removed.

Tocqueville says that the march of equality is providential and that democracy lies in everyone's future.[16] But there is a great difference between his assertion of a broad, centuries-long historical trend toward democracy and the belief that a stable democracy can be established at a given place and time. Tocqueville spent a great deal of time explaining why democracy worked better in the United States than in his native France, based on the existence of what are now called "supporting structures" from the realms of culture and social practice. Thus a Straussian understanding of the importance of regime implied both that regime change was necessary to bring about certain changes in behavior and that it was extremely difficult to achieve.

ALBERT WOHLSTETTER

Leo Strauss said virtually nothing about foreign policy, however much students or students of students may have sought to translate his philosophical ideas into policies. The same cannot be said for Albert Wohlstetter, on the other hand, who was the teacher of Paul Wolfowitz, Richard Perle, Zalmay Khalilzad, and other people in or close to the Bush administration.

Wohlstetter was a mathematical logician who worked at the Rand Corporation in its glory days in the 1950s and later taught at the University of Chicago. His career was marked by a long-standing concern with two central issues. The first was the problem of extended deterrence. Wohlstetter argued against the belief, promoted in early Cold War days by strategists like the French general Pierre Galois, that a minimum nuclear deterrent would be a cheap and effective form of national defense. Wohlstetter was best known in public policy circles for his 1954 Rand bomber-basing study, which demonstrated the vulnerability of U.S. intermediate-range nuclear bombers around the periphery of the USSR to preemptive attack. Simply having a nuclear deterrent was not sufficient; countries had to worry about their vulnerability in nuclear warfighting scenarios. This study established the concept of first strike/second strike that became a staple of Cold War deterrence theory.[17]

The second of Wohlstetter's long-standing concerns was nuclear proliferation. He was skeptical about the way the nonproliferation regime that grew up in the wake of the 1968 Nonproliferation Treaty (NPT) enshrined a right to civilian nuclear power while trying to prevent the spread of nuclear weapons; the two types of technologies, according to him, could not be verifiably separated. Many of Wohlstetter's fears are being played out today in the Middle East, where Iran has asserted a right under the NPT to produce enriched uranium for civilian nuclear energy, a procedure that provides excellent cover for a covert nuclear weapons program.

The issue of nuclear proliferation was linked, in Wohlstetter's mind, with that of extended deterrence. For though it might be conceivable that a world with many nuclear states might be made stable through mutual deterrence, this would not happen unless those states achieved secure second-strike capabilities. Small, nascent nuclear forces were much more likely to promote instability by tempting opponents to preemptive measures.

It is not clear whether Albert Wohlstetter ever came to regard himself as a neoconservative, but he and his students merged more or less seamlessly with this movement because of his dark view of the threat posed by the Soviet Union. He did not accept the received wisdom of the 1960s and 1970s that mutual assured destruction (MAD) would be sufficient to deter the Soviet Union. Wohlstetter argued that the threat to wipe out tens or hundreds of millions of civilians was both immoral and noncredible. He noted that with increasing ICBM accuracies and the deployment of multiple warheads, a so-called counterforce war might one day become thinkable—for example, if the Soviets launched a first strike on American nuclear bases, wiping out the bulk of U.S. land-based nuclear forces and holding back enough weapons to deter a submarine-based counterstrike on cities.

Although most counterforce scenarios would probably also bring about the deaths of millions of people on both sides, through fallout and other secondary effects, such a war was at least thinkable, as opposed to countervalue wars of nuclear annihilation that targeted cities. Wohlstetter argued that the Soviet Union had accepted casualties on that scale for political ends in the past and therefore might not always be deterred by a force posture vulnerable to a counterforce attack in the future.

Wohlstetter, Wolfowitz, Perle, and political allies like Senator Henry M. "Scoop" Jackson (as well as former officials like Paul Nitze, who worked with Wolfowitz on the so-called Team B that scrutinized the Soviet threat) were aligned against Henry Kissinger and centrist Republicans and Democrats who sought to use strategic arms control to enshrine MAD. They criticized the SALT treaty on strategic nuclear weapons negotiated in the 1970s for failing to constrain growing Soviet counterforce capabilities, thereby weakening deterrence.

Wohlstetter thus shared with the older neoconservatives a jaundiced view of the Soviet Union, and with them and the Strauss students a belief that regimes mattered to foreign policy. What he brought to the table that they did not was an expertise on international relations, defense policy, and security issues. During the late 1970s and 1980s, Wohlstetter turned his attention to the Persian Gulf, Iraq, the Iran-Iraq war, and the burgeoning problem of nuclear proliferation in the Middle East. He and his students thus played a critical role in translating a broad, general set of neoconservative ideas into specific foreign policy preferences. Through Wohlstetter's influence on people like Robert Bartley, the long-time *Wall Street Journal* opinion page editor, these preferences came to define the hard-line alternative to Kissinger and détente and were incorporated into policy when Ronald Reagan was elected president.

A constant thread running throughout Wohlstetter's work was the impact on warfare of increasing targeting precision. At the nuclear level, multiple independently targetable reentry vehicles (MIRVs) made possible a counterforce strike at hardened missile silos, while in conventional warfare precision targeting made obsolete the need to flatten entire cities and their civilian populations as occurred during the Allied bombing campaigns against Germany and Japan. Wohlstetter thought of this precision targeting as more humane than the warfare that in the Second World War claimed the lives of hundreds of thousands of innocent civilians in cities like Dresden, Hamburg, Tokyo, and Hiroshima.

But the actual emergence of precision targeting in conventional warfare had some unanticipated results. By the 1990s, the technological revolution that Wohlstetter foresaw so brilliantly had largely come about. From the first Gulf War on, Americans became familiar with video footage of American bombs streaking toward their targets and blowing up individual buildings or vehicles. Aging B-52 bombers armed with JDAMs (the Joint Direct Attack Munition that turned "dumb" bombs into precisely targeted ones) became a staple of the Afghan war, where they could be called forth from the sky by Special Forces troops riding horses with Northern Alliance fighters. These developments, plus a parallel revolution in information and communications technology, made possible a vast transformation in the way that warfare could be conducted.

This shift toward a lighter, faster, and more mobile form of combat, strongly promoted by Secretary of Defense Donald Rumsfeld as military "transformation," also made American intervention more likely. It created a sense that war would be low-cost from the standpoint of American casualties. The 1991 Gulf War produced fewer than two hundred combat deaths; the numerous small interventions of the Clinton administration in places like Haiti and Bosnia culminated in the 1999 Kosovo war, in which not a single American died. Rumsfeld seemed to want to invade Iraq with the smallest possible force structure to demonstrate the feasibility of this new kind of warfare.

It is, of course, better for the United States if fewer Americans die in war. On the other hand, the success of American military technology during the 1990s created the illusion that military intervention would always be as clean or cheap as the Gulf or Kosovo wars. The Iraq war has clearly demonstrated the limits of this form of light, mobile warfare: it can defeat virtually any existing conventional military force, but it provides no special advantages in fighting a prolonged insurgency. JDAMs and television-guided antitank missiles cannot distinguish between insurgents and noncombatants or help soldiers speak Arabic. Indeed, the very model of a professional, all-volunteer military that was established in Vietnam's waning days works only for short, high-intensity wars. If the United States were serious about regime change and the use of its military to promote political goals in countries around the world, it would need a military different in many ways from the one envisioned by Albert Wohlstetter.

The Great Merge

The founding fathers of the neoconservative movement, Kristol, Bell, and Glazer, ended up in different places politically. Whereas Kristol embraced the Reagan Revolution and became a Republican, Bell and Glazer were more centrist and less partisan. Daniel Patrick Moynihan remained a Democrat and voted, as senator from New York, against the 1996 welfare reform bill.

Given the origins of the movement in left-wing anticommunism, it is not surprising that neoconservatives would for the most part end up opposing the realist foreign policy of Henry Kissinger during the 1970s. Realism, as defined in international relations theory, begins with the premise that all nations, regardless of regime, struggle for power. Realism can at times become relativistic and agnostic about regimes; realists by and large do not believe that liberal democracy is a potentially universal form of government or that the human values underlying it are necessarily superior to those underlying nondemocratic societies. Indeed, they tend to warn against crusading democratic idealism, which in their view can become dangerously destabilizing.

Henry Kissinger was a classical realist, a position he held consistently from his doctoral dissertation on Metternich to his magnum opus on diplomacy.[18] His attempt, as national security advisor and then as secretary of state, to seek détente with the former Soviet Union reflected his view that the latter was a permanent fixture in world affairs. The United States and other democracies would have to learn to accommodate themselves, according to

Kissinger, to its power. It is thus not surprising that most neo-conservatives were broadly supportive of Ronald Reagan's effort to remoralize the struggle between Soviet communism and liberal democracy and did not wince in embarrassment when he spoke of the Soviet Union as an "evil empire."

On the other hand, from the late 1970s on it became increasingly hard to disentangle neoconservatism from other, more traditional varieties of American conservatism, whether based on small-government libertarianism, religious or social conservatism, or American nationalism. Even identifying who qualified as a neoconservative became difficult. This was true for two reasons. First, many neoconservative ideas were wholeheartedly adopted by mainstream conservatives and, indeed, by a broader American public. Ronald Reagan may have offered anecdotes of "welfare queens," but the debate about welfare turned much more serious when the link between social programs like AFDC and welfare dependency was supported by empirical social scientists in the pages of *The Public Interest*. In foreign policy, hard-nosed Cold Warriors like Paul Nitze found themselves aligned with the neoconservatives in their opposition to Kissinger's accommodation of the USSR.

But the second reason for this convergence was that many neoconservatives began adopting domestic policy positions of traditional conservatives. It is safe to say that there was no natural affinity between the original views of the CCNY/*Public Interest* crowd—most started out, after all, as socialists—and the free market conservatism of Ronald Reagan.[19] And yet by the 1980s most neoconservatives had made their peace with American capitalism: they were not true believers like the followers of Ludwig von Mises or Friedrich Hayek, but they never put a critique of market capitalism at the top of their agenda. By the 1990s, this convergence would extend to the sphere of culture and religion. Neoconservatives, however, remained distinct from Jacksonian conservatives like Patrick Buchanan on issues like immigration and free trade (both of which the former largely supported).[20]

The intertwining of neoconservatism with other strands of American conservatism made it hard to identify specifically neoconservative positions. Neoconservatism's contemporary enemies vastly overstate the uniformity of views that has existed within the group of self-identified neoconservatives since the 1980s. Their lack of uniformity became particularly prevalent after the unexpected demise of communism in 1989–91, when unity on foreign policy evaporated and neoconservatives began debating among themselves the nature of American national interests in the post–Cold War world.

I argued above that a belief in the importance of the nature of the regime and hostility to the implicit relativism of realism united most neoconservatives. But in the early 1990s there was no agreement among neoconservatives on the extent to which democracy promotion or human rights should underlie U.S. foreign policy, or the appropriate degree of American engagement around the world. The *National Interest* editor Owen Harries, who published many neoconservative authors, was himself a self-proclaimed realist (and an Australian national) who argued for a narrower understanding of U.S. interests. Irving Kristol began arguing in the 1980s that the United States ought to consider disengaging from Europe; his founding of a magazine entitled *The National Interest* suggested a more restrictive view of how America should see itself in the world. There was active debate among self-styled neoconservatives on most of the major foreign policy issues that arose during the 1990s, such as U.S.-China relations, NATO expansion, and whether to intervene in the Balkans.

KRISTOL, KAGAN, AND THE 1990S

The expansive, interventionist, democracy-promoting position that has come to be seen today as the essence of neoconservatism—what Max Boot labels "hard Wilsonianism"[21] and others "Wilsonianism on steroids"—is much more the product of younger writers like Irving Kristol's son William and of Robert Kagan, who began arguing for this kind of foreign policy in the pages of William Kristol's magazine *The Weekly Standard* during the mid- to late-1990s. The Kristol-Kagan effort to redefine neoconservatism in this fashion has been immensely successful, insofar as most people around the world now perceive it this way; such people will not be persuaded to change their minds regardless of the facts about the diverse views of actual neoconservatives.

The Kristol-Kagan effort to refine neoconservative foreign policy was first laid out systematically in a 1996 article they wrote for *Foreign Affairs* (expanded into a book entitled *Present Dangers* [2000]) defining a "neo-Reaganite" agenda for the Republican Party. They took issue with Jeane Kirkpatrick's brief for a return to American "normalcy" after the end of the Cold War and called instead for "benevolent hegemony" under American leadership, a policy that entailed "resisting, and where possible undermining, rising dictators and hostile ideologies; . . . supporting American interests and liberal democratic principles; and . . . providing assistance to those struggling against the more extreme manifestations of human evil."[22]

This neo-Reaganite foreign policy has often been described as Wilsonian, but it was Wilsonianism minus international institutions.[23] That is, Woodrow Wilson sought to establish a democratic peace and promote the spread of liberal democracy through the creation of a liberal international legal order based on the League of Nations. This tradition of liberal internationalism continued as a strong component of American foreign policy through the efforts of the Roosevelt and Truman administrations to found the United Nations, but was completely absent from either the older or the newer neoconservative agendas. In place of international institutions, Kristol and Kagan emphasized three tools for projecting U.S. influence: overwhelming military superiority; a renewed dedication to U.S. alliances; and missile defense as a means of protecting the American homeland from counterattack.[24]

Kristol and Kagan argued explicitly for regime change as a

central component of their neo-Reaganite policy. They asserted
that getting tyrannical regimes to play by civilized rules through
agreements, international law, or norms was ultimately unwork-
able, and that in the long run only democratization could ensure
compliance and converging interests. It was a mistake, they said,
for the United States not to have gone on to Baghdad during the
1991 Gulf War to remove Saddam Hussein, while NATO forces
should have moved beyond Kosovo to topple Miloševiç in Serbia. They called for regime change not only in the case of "rogue"
states like Iraq, North Korea, and Iran, but also for China, which
in the period before September 11 constituted their central op-
ponent in the international system.

The Kristol-Kagan agenda was driven by a belief that this
kind of activist foreign policy was in the best interests of the
United States. But it was also driven by a less obvious political
calculation. During the Clinton years, when the United States
did not seem to be facing any serious external threats, David
Brooks, then an editor at the *Weekly Standard*, began advocat-
ing pursuit of a policy of "national greatness," taking the administration of Theodore Roosevelt as a model.[25] National greatness
was seen as an antidote to the small- or anti-government libertarianism of one important wing of the Republican Party, the
wing that had been isolationist up through the Second World
War and might turn in that direction again. This might be seen
as part of a broader tendency among Americans, first noted by
Alexis de Tocqueville, to turn away from public affairs toward

a narrow-minded preoccupation with a small circle of family and friends.

National greatness inevitably manifests itself through foreign policy, since foreign policy is always a public matter and involves issues of life and death. In addition, Kristol noted on several occasions that the Republican Party always did better when foreign policy issues were at stake than when the focus was on domestic policy or the economy. They thus designed a foreign policy around a very abstract view of domestic politics—that America needed a national project to get its mind off issues like the stock market boom and Monica Lewinsky—rather than deriving the foreign policy from the nature of the outside world.

The Kristol-Kagan agenda put them at odds with important factions within the Republican Party during the late 1990s. Their "hard" Wilsonianism converged instead with many of the policies of the Clinton administration: they supported humanitarian intervention in the Balkans and Africa and argued for a level of international activism that was anathema to both the Kissingerian-realist and Jacksonian-nationalist wings of the party. It also put them at odds with many other self-styled neoconservatives like Jeane Kirkpatrick and Charles Krauthammer, who at the time had much more restrictive views of American national interests.

One feature of neoconservative writing during the 1990s was its general lack of interest in international economics or development. Much recent demand for new international institutions has been driven by the requirements of global trade and investment, which has led to formation of bodies like the General Agreement on Tariffs and Trades (GATT), the World Trade Organization (WTO), the World Intellectual Property Organization, and the like. Neoconservatives were by and large concerned with politics, security, and ideology; they generated relatively few distinctive opinions about globalization, competitiveness, development, and other issues. Articles in neoconservative journals on economic subjects tended to be delegated to professional economists. Despite some early theoretical critiques of modern capitalism, economic policy prescriptions over time increasingly tended to track the orthodoxy of contemporary American neoclassical economics.[26]

Because the Kristol-Kagan agenda has become so indelibly associated with neoconservatism and was put into practice by the administration of George W. Bush, it is an uphill struggle to try to redefine neoconservative foreign policy after the fact. But it should be clear that the neoconservative heritage was a complex one that had multiple strands, and that the specific policy implications for how to deal with China, Iraq, or the Europeans that one could derive from the underlying principles were not necessarily those chosen by Kristol and Kagan.

WAS RONALD REAGAN A NEOCONSERVATIVE? IS GEORGE W. BUSH?

The intertwining of neoconservatives with the mainstream conservative movement in America from the 1980s on raises some interesting questions about who qualifies as a neoconservative. Kristol and Kagan explicitly claimed the mantle of Reaganism and sought to derive their foreign policy from his. To what extent is the foreign policy of George W. Bush simply a continuation of the tradition of Reaganism, and, to that extent, does it qualify President Bush as a neoconservative?

On one level, it seems somewhat odd to call either Reagan or Bush a neoconservative. Neoconservatives were in their origin (mostly) Jewish intellectuals who loved to read, write, argue, and debate; in a sense, it was their intellectual brilliance, their ability to reflect, and the nuance and flexibility associated with intellectual debate that was most notable about them, and what set them apart from the paleoconservatives.

Of the two presidents in question, Ronald Reagan in my view more clearly qualifies as a neoconservative. Much as his enemies are loath to admit it, Ronald Reagan was an intellectual of sorts: in the first decade or so of his career, all he had to offer were ideas and arguments about communism and the free market, American values, and the defects of the reigning liberal orthodoxy. He also bore a similarity to the City College crowd insofar as he came to anticommunism from the left: he started out as a Democrat and an admirer of Franklin Roosevelt and was a labor leader as president of the Screen Actors Guild. His insight about the nature of communism seems to have arisen as a result of his struggles with communists or communist sympathizers in Hollywood. His foreign policy was clearly distinct from that of Jimmy

Carter or the Nixon-Ford-Kissinger team. He believed firmly that the internal character of regimes defines their external behavior and was initially unwilling to compromise with the Soviet Union because he saw more clearly than most its internal contradictions and weaknesses.[27]

On the question of whether George W. Bush is, or ever was, a neoconservative, it seems to me that by the beginning of his second term he had become one. As a candidate, he spoke relatively little about a Wilsonian agenda in foreign policy and famously argued in 2000, "I don't think our troops ought to be used for what's called nation-building. I think our troops ought to be used to fight and win war." His foreign policy confidante and future national security advisor and secretary of state Condoleezza Rice complained that "U.S. troops should not be used to escort school-children" in the Balkans, urging that they be brought home. The early justifications for the war in Iraq were not couched primarily in Wilsonian terms but in terms of the threat from Iraqi WMD and Iraq's connection to terrorism. President Bush systematically addressed the larger agenda of political transformation only in the month immediately preceding the war, when he formally introduced the idea of democratizing Iraq as a war aim, as well as the larger project of politically transforming the Middle East.[28]

By the time of his second inaugural, Bush had come to accept much of the neoconservative agenda as at least the rhetorical framework for his new term. He said nothing about terrorism and little about security, speaking instead of the universality of democratic values ("Eventually the call of freedom comes to every mind and every soul"). He linked internal regime with external behavior (promoting democracy "is the urgent requirement of our nation's security") and noted that "the survival of liberty in our land increasingly depends on the success of liberty in other lands."

Many commentators noted that Bush came to putting the Wilsonian agenda front and center largely because the security rationale for the defining act of his administration—the Iraq war—had disappeared. That may be true, but once the policy was in place it did not matter how the president got there. And there is little doubt that Bush believes in what he says about the importance of the democracy-promotion agenda, at least as a matter of principle. The problem for Bush's second term is that the policies undertaken during his first term generated so much hostility to his administration that he managed to discredit the perfectly fine agenda of democracy promotion even as he himself was coming to it. His ex-post effort to justify a preventive war in idealistic terms has led many critics to simply desire the opposite of whatever he wants.

A Balance Sheet

Now that the very word *neoconservative* has become a term of abuse, we need to look at the neoconservative legacy, not of the past five years, but of the past fifty.

As noted above, there is a great deal of diversity in the views held by self-styled neoconservatives for the past quarter-century, and nothing approaching a party line. Nonetheless, it is possible to extract four basic principles or themes characterizing neo-conservative thought that logically explain the policy positions they have taken and distinguish neoconservatives from the other schools of thought about foreign policy. These principles are:

- A belief that the internal character of regimes matters and that foreign policy must reflect the deepest values of liberal democratic societies. The view that the nature of the regime matters to external behavior is held much more consistently by neoconservatives than the alternative realist view that all states seek power regardless of regime type. The early neoconservative anti-Stalinists saw the Cold War as a struggle over ideology and values, a fight that continued into the Reagan years over how to deal with the Soviet Union. The Straussian current in neoconservatism also saw the regime as a central organizing principle of politics.

- A belief that American power has been and could be used for moral purposes, and that the United States needs to remain engaged in international affairs. There is a realist dimension to neoconservative foreign policy, which lies in the understanding that power is often necessary to achieve moral purposes. As the world's dominant power, the United States has special responsibilities in the realm of security. This was true in the Balkans

in the 1990s, as it was in World War II and the fight
against Hitler.

- A distrust of ambitious social engineering projects. The
  untoward consequences of ambitious efforts at social
  planning is a consistent theme in neoconservative
  thought that links the critique of Stalinism in the 1940s
  with *The Public Interest*'s skepticism about the Great Society in the 1960s.

- And finally, skepticism about the legitimacy and effectiveness of international law and institutions to achieve
  either security or justice. While neoconservatives have
  been labeled Wilsonian, Woodrow Wilson himself
  sought to promote democracy through the creation of
  the League of Nations. The dream that power politics
  could be transcended and replaced by international law
  is shared today by American liberal internationalists and
  many Europeans. The neoconservatives in this respect
  agree with the realists that international law is too weak
  to enforce rules and restrain aggression; they are highly
  critical of the United Nations as either an arbiter or
  an enforcer of international justice. Distrust of the
  United Nations does not, for most neoconservatives,
  extend to all forms of multilateral cooperation; most are
  favorably disposed to the NATO alliance, for example,
  and believe in collective action based on shared democratic principles.[29]

On the central issue that defined them, the global struggle against communism, neoconservatives were more correct than their opponents in their fundamental analysis of the nature of the problem and its solutions—indeed, more correct than many neoconservatives themselves realized. In the early days of the Cold War, a wide spectrum of Americans, from John F. Kennedy and Hubert Humphrey to Paul Nitze and George Kennan, believed that communist totalitarianism represented a unique kind of evil. Although they did not use the term "regime change," many early Cold Warriors assumed that the Soviet challenge grew out of the nature of the regime and would not end until the regime itself was replaced.

After Vietnam, however, a very different view emerged that was reflected in the words of President Jimmy Carter, who believed that the West lived in "inordinate fear of Communism." The latter position was shared by people on the left who had some sympathy for the socialist aims of communism and disagreed only with the means, and by realists on the right who accepted communism as another form of government to which Western democracies would have to accommodate themselves. Neoconservatives after Vietnam simply continued to bear the torch of the earlier Cold War view about communism as a unique evil.

Ronald Reagan was ridiculed by sophisticated people on the American left and in Europe for labeling the Soviet Union and its allies an "evil empire" and for challenging Mikhail Gorbachev not just to reform his system but to "tear down this wall." His assistant secretary of defense for international security policy, Richard Perle, was denounced as the "prince of darkness" for this uncompromising, hard-line position; and his proposal for a double zero in the intermediate-range nuclear forces negotiations (that is, the complete elimination of medium-range missiles) was attacked as hopelessly out of touch by the *bien pensant* centrist foreign policy experts at places like the Council on Foreign Relations and the State Department. That community felt that the Reaganites were dangerously utopian in their hopes for actually winning, as opposed to managing, the Cold War.[30]

And yet victory in the Cold War is exactly what happened in 1989–91. Gorbachev accepted not only the double zero but deep cuts in conventional forces; he then failed to stop the Polish, Hungarian, and East German defections from the empire. Communism collapsed within a couple of years because of its internal moral weaknesses and contradictions, and with regime change in Eastern Europe and the former Soviet Union the Warsaw Pact threat to the West evaporated.[31] Former subjects of the evil empire like the Poles, Czechs, and Estonians had no quarrel with Reagan's moralistic language, and to this day they resent the willingness of so many in Western Europe to abandon the cause of their liberation from Soviet power during the Cold War. The current divisions between old and new Europe can be directly traced to the issue of regime change: the new Europeans knew that their situation would not fundamentally change until they could rejoin the democratic West.

The borders of NATO have now been extended to the Gulf of Bothnia and the Oder River, and the popular upsurge in Ukraine that brought Viktor Yushchenko to power in 2004–5 suggests that the democratic wave may not be over. The rapid, unexpected, and largely peaceful collapse of communism validated the concept of regime change as an approach to international relations. And yet this extraordinary vindication laid the groundwork for the wrong turn taken by many neoconservatives in the decade following that has had direct consequences for their management of post–September 11 foreign policy. The problem was twofold, occurring both on the level of their interpretation of what had happened in 1989 and in their psychological relationship to their political opponents.

Nineteen eighty-nine was an annus mirabilis, a political miracle that not even Ronald Reagan, who thought communism was headed for the "dust bin of history," could possibly have anticipated. Virtually every student of Soviet power, whether on the left or the right, assumed that regime change would not come to Eastern Europe peacefully and with apparent Soviet sanction. Everyone assumed that politburos in Poland and East Germany, as well as in Moscow, were split between reformers and hardliners, and that when frontally challenged the latter would dig in their heels and resist change with military force. That the hardliners themselves had no stomach for such a struggle suggested a much deeper moral rot at the heart of the communist system than practically anyone had suspected.[32]

One can react to a miracle in one of two ways. One can say, "miracles happen," and dramatically raise one's expectations for their repetition across the board. In the case of the collapse of communism, this attitude appeared in the universalization of the experience of the East Europeans to other parts of the world. The East Europeans clearly did seek liberation from an evil tyranny; the elimination of Soviet power was like the bursting of a dam that allowed a river to return to its natural bed. We had been fooled once by people who said that the East Europeans had learned to love their captivity; by this view, we should not underestimate the democratic impulse elsewhere.

The second reaction is to thank the Lord for one's extraordinary luck, pocket one's earnings, and reflect on the uniqueness of the circumstances of what one has just witnessed. One can believe that liberal democracy constitutes the wave of the future without believing that fearsome tyrannies will inevitably crumble with scarcely a shot fired. With the benefit of 20/20 hindsight, we can see that communism was a uniquely hollow and artificial ideology that grew no organic roots in the underlying societies. The return of the East Europeans to democracy had much to do with the fact that they were in fact Europeans at a high level of development whose natural progress had been arrested by the horrible events of the twentieth century. But this does not imply that all dictatorships similarly lack social roots or would disappear as quickly or as peacefully as did European communism.

Many people interpret my book *The End of History and the Last*

Man (1992) as arguing in favor of the first interpretation: that there is a universal hunger for liberty in all people that will inevitably lead them to liberal democracy, and that we are living in the midst of an accelerating, transnational movement in favor of liberal democracy. This is a misreading of the argument.[33] *The End of History* is finally an argument about modernization. What is *initially* universal is not the desire for liberal democracy but rather the desire to live in a modern society, with its technology, high standards of living, health care, and access to the wider world. Economic modernization, when successful, tends to drive demands for political participation by creating a middle class with property to protect, higher levels of education, and greater concern for their recognition as individuals. Liberal democracy is one of the by-products of this modernization process, something that *becomes* a universal aspiration only in the course of historical time. I never posited a strong version of modernization theory, with rigid stages of development or economically determined outcomes. Contingency, leadership, and ideas always played a complicating role, which made major setbacks possible if not likely.

The scholar Ken Jowitt has described my views and the way they differed from the Bush administration's approach accurately:

> Initially, if implicitly, the Bush administration subscribed to the "end of history" thesis that the "rest" of the world would more or less naturally become like the West in gen-

eral and the United States in particular. September 11 changed that. In its aftermath, the Bush administration has concluded that Fukuyama's historical timetable is too laissez-faire and not nearly attentive enough to the levers of historical change. History, the Bush administration has concluded, needs deliberate organization, leadership, and direction. In this irony of ironies, the Bush administration's identification of regime change as critical to its anti-terrorist policy and integral to its desire for a democratic capitalist world has led to an active "Leninist" foreign policy in place of Fukuyama's passive "Marxist" social teleology.[34]

I did not like the original version of Leninism and was skeptical when the Bush administration turned Leninist. Democracy in my view is likely to expand universally *in the long run*. But whether the rapid and relatively peaceful transition to democracy and free markets made by the Poles, Hungarians, or even the Romanians can be quickly replicated in other parts of the world, or promoted through the application of power by outsiders at any given point in history, is open to doubt.

Within the former communist world, there has been a wide variance in transition outcomes, ranging from a rapid shift to democracy and market economy in the cases of Poland and Estonia to survival of authoritarian government in the cases of Belarus and many of the Central Asian successor states. Leaders, history, culture, geography, and other contextual factors varied across the former communist world and greatly affected the success of political change. As will be discussed below, democratic transitions are in general difficult to bring about, and economic development is equally hard to foster. This suggests that explosive transformations of the sort we saw in the communist world that brought the Cold War to an end are likely to be exceptions rather than the rule.

Neoconservatives like Kristol and Kagan interpreted events differently. In *Present Dangers*, they wrote:

To many the idea of America using its power to promote changes of regime in nations ruled by dictators rings of utopianism. But in fact, it is eminently realistic. There is something perverse in declaring the impossibility of promoting democratic change abroad in light of the record of the past three decades. After we have already seen dictatorships toppled by democratic forces in such unlikely places as the Philippines, Indonesia, Chile, Nicaragua, Paraguay, Taiwan and South Korea, how utopian is it to imagine a change of regime in a place like Iraq? How utopian is it to work for the fall of the Communist Party oligarchy in China after a far more powerful and, arguably, more stable such oligarchy fell in the Soviet Union? With democratic change sweeping the world at an unprecedented rate over these past thirty years, is it "realist" to insist that no further victories can be won?[35]

This belief in the imminence of democratic change was based on two things. The first had to do with an interpretation of the underlying cross-cultural appeal of democracy and with the contagiousness of the democratic idea at the end of the twentieth century. The second had to do with their belief in the centrality of American power and, in particular, the view that Ronald Reagan's policies had been critical to the demise of the former Soviet Union.

It is clear that a contagious wave of democratic fervor swept over many parts of the world in the late 1980s and early 1990s; how else can we explain the series of democratic transitions that occurred in sub-Saharan Africa in the early 1990s, a region that met none of the structural conditions for successful democracy? But a theory of democratic change emerging out of a broad process of modernization like the one laid out in *The End of History* suggests that democratic contagion can take a society only so far; if certain structural conditions are not met, instability and setback are in store. This explains why all previous waves of democratization eventually receded and went into reverse, and there was no reason to think that the same thing would not eventually happen to what Samuel Huntington labeled the Third Wave of democratization that began in the mid-1970s. By the first decade of the twenty-first century, there was growing evidence that the Third Wave had indeed crested. New democracies failed to consolidate in Haiti, Cambodia, and Belarus; Moldova and Ukraine were foundering in corruption; and established democracies faced setbacks in Venezuela, Bolivia, Ecuador, and Peru, while Argentina's liberalizing reforms met with an economic crisis in 2001. Russia under President Vladimir Putin was clearly moving to undo many of the liberal reforms of the Yeltsin era, while many of Africa's democratic experiments proved fleeting (most notoriously, that of Zimbabwe). Although democratic elections were held in many countries by the 1990s, liberal rule of law and observance of human rights made much less progress and in many cases suffered serious setbacks. Thomas Carothers, a student of democracy promotion, has argued that the commonly held view of the 1990s that most countries in the world were at various points in a "transition to democracy" was wrong; many parts of the former communist world were not transitioning anywhere but were stuck in a semi-authoritarian gray zone.[36]

There is no existing theory that explains how democratic waves start in the first place, or why and when they crest or recede. The democratic revolutions in Serbia, Georgia, and Ukraine in the early twenty-first century suggest that there is still considerable momentum left in the former communist world. But while there is nothing wrong with being hopeful and open to the possibility of miracles, it is another thing altogether to predicate a foreign policy on the *likelihood* of multiple near-term democratic transitions.

What Jowitt labels the Leninist view that history could be accelerated through American agency was rooted in a specific interpretation of the end of the Cold War: namely, that it had been "won" by the Reagan administration through the buildup of the American military. This interpretation, questionable in itself, should have been of limited relevance to the situation in Iraq.

There is no doubt that Reagan's principled anticommunism offered hope to people in Eastern Europe and indeed in Russia itself, which is why he remains a hero in places like Poland. It is also the case that the U.S. buildup played a role in convincing Soviet leaders that they would have difficulty competing with the United States. But an event as massive as the collapse of the former USSR had many causes, some deeply embedded in the nature of the Soviet system (for example, the illegitimacy of the governing ideology) and others accidental and contingent (the untimely death of Yuri Andropov and the rise of Mikhail Gorbachev). Conservatives of all stripes tend to put too much emphasis on the American military buildup as the cause of the USSR's collapse, when political and economic factors were at least as important. Scholars John Ikenberry and Daniel Deudney have argued that the attractive "pull" of the West, and Soviet awareness that partnership with the West was possible, were at least as important in explaining the Soviet collapse.[37] In any event, to the extent that military policy was important in explaining the Soviet Union's collapse, it was a policy of containment and deterrence rather than rollback.

There was also a psychological dimension to the way many neoconservatives reacted to the end of the Cold War. During much of the Cold War neoconservatives became used to being a small, despised minority. Although many of their ideas were finally put into practice in the Reagan administration, it remained the case that the foreign policy establishment—the people who ran the bureaucracies at the State Department, the intelligence community, and the Pentagon, as well as the legions of advisers, think-tank specialists, and academics—was largely dismissive of them. Neoconservatives were also used to having the Europeans look down on them as moralistic naïfs, reckless cowboys, or worse. They were used to bucking conventional wisdom and going for solutions—like the double zero or the tearing down of the Berlin Wall—that everyone else thought were completely out of the realm of possibility.

The sudden collapse of communism vindicated many of these ideas and made them appear mainstream and obvious after 1989. This naturally did a great deal to bolster the self-confidence of those who had held them, a self-confidence that strongly reinforced the us-versus-them solidarity that characterizes all groups of like-minded people. Bureaucratic battles tend to strengthen proclivities toward group solidarity natural to all human beings in ways that have to be experienced to be fully understood. This was all the more so given the stakes of the ideological battles during the close of the Cold War.

Great leadership often involves putting aside self-doubt, bucking conventional wisdom, and listening only to an inner voice that tells you the right thing to do. That is the essence of strong character. The problem is that bad leadership can also flow from these same characteristics: steely determination can become stubbornness; the willingness to flout conventional wisdom can amount to a lack of common sense; the inner voice can become delusional. The fact that one was proven unexpectedly right under a surprising set of circumstances does not necessarily mean that one will be right the next time around. It probably does mean, however, that one will be psychologically handicapped in recognizing that one is wrong in future cases.

After their return to power in 2001, proponents of the war in the Pentagon and vice president's office became excessively distrustful of anyone who did not share their views, a distrust that extended to Secretary of State Colin Powell and much of the intelligence community. Bureaucratic tribalism exists in all administrations, but it rose to poisonous levels in Bush's first term. Team loyalty trumped open-minded discussion, and was directly responsible for the administration's failure to plan adequately for the period after the end of active combat.

After Neoconservatism

The four neoconservative principles listed above have been widely shared not only by neoconservatives but by other important groups across the spectrum of American political life. The principle of a democracy-based and internationalist foreign policy is held in common with much of the Democratic Party; the belief in the ultimate moral purposes of American power and skepticism about international institutions are both realist ideas; and the pessimism about social engineering is shared with the conventional Right. Put together in a single package, however, they represent a distinctive approach to foreign policy.

As noted in Chapter 1, however, these abstract principles were interpreted after the Cold War in particular ways that produced judgments that were biased in certain systematic directions. These biases might be good or bad depending on the nature of the outside world; as it turned out, they became the basis for what I regard as a number of missteps by the Bush administration.

Neoconservatives after the collapse of communism tended to overestimate the level of threat facing the United States. During the Cold War, they rightly (in my view) took a dark view of the challenge posed by the Soviet Union, regarding it both as a military threat and as a moral evil. After the breakup of the USSR, when the United States emerged as the world's sole superpower, many neoconservatives continued to see the world as populated by dangerous and underappreciated threats.[38] Some saw China, by the late 1990s, as the new great power rival, a position from which it was rescued only by the September 11 attacks. The al-Qaida threat was real enough, of course, and nobody needed to invent new enemies for the United States. But the terrorist threat was merged with the rogue state/proliferation threat in a way that made it seem utterly apocalyptic. The preventive-war doctrine, and the significantly higher level of risks it entailed, were reasonable responses only if one accepted these expansive premises about the nature of the threat.

Neoconservatives, like most Americans, from the beginning had a strong sense of the potentially moral uses of American power, which has been employed throughout the republic's history to fight tyranny and expand democracy around the world. But belief in the possibility of linking power and morality was transformed into a tremendous overemphasis on the role of power, specifically military power, as a means of achieving American national purposes.

The decision to use force sooner rather than later, or to emphasize hard over soft power, is typically a matter of prudence rather than principle. Yet the officials who populated the Bush administration, as well as their outside supporters, were more likely to have focused throughout their careers on high-intensity combat rather than post-conflict reconstruction, or defense budgets rather than development assistance, as policy issues. No one was opposed in principle to the use of soft power; they simply hadn't thought about it very much. As the saying goes, when your only tool is a hammer, all problems look like nails.

Excessively optimistic assumptions about post-Saddam Iraq set the stage for the failure to think through the requirements of post-conflict security and nation-building. Regime change was conceived not as a matter of the slow and painstaking construction of liberal and democratic institutions but simply as the negative task of getting rid of the old regime. The bias in favor of high-tech military power as the chief policy instrument continues to this day: while the *Weekly Standard* has turned against Donald Rumsfeld and called for his resignation, its chief criticism of him remains his failure to provide enough troops to secure Iraq, rather than the multiple other dimensions of nation-building where U.S. policy fell short.

Neoconservatives share with realists a skepticism about the ability of international law and institutions to solve serious security problems, a skepticism that was greatly reinforced by the experience of the Cold War. But disdain for the opinions of the "international community" as embodied by the United Nations broadened into a disdain for virtually any country that did not positively support the Bush administration's policies. During the Cold War, neoconservatives were determined Atlanticists who argued that the Soviet Union represented a threat to the common freedoms shared by Europeans and Americans. Neoconservatives in the 1990s continued to argue that they were in favor of multilateralism if it involved countries that were genuine democracies, that is, NATO. But when it became clear that NATO would not support the Iraq intervention, neoconservatives lost any interest in working through it. By the time the war began, America's European allies came to be increasingly demonized as anti-American, anti-Semitic, or somehow imperfectly democratic. Multilateralism was reduced to accepting help from only those who offered it on American terms: "coalitions of the willing."

Skepticism about international law and the fight with the Europeans over Iraq has meant that neoconservatives have had virtually nothing innovative or interesting to say about new possibilities for multilateral organization. They would much rather harp on the United Nation's failings in the Oil for Food scandal than think about how to create an organization of democracies that would build incentives to improve governance and democracy around the world. In the period immediately after World War II, American power was used not just to deter Soviet aggression but also to create a welter of new international organizations and agreements, from the Bretton Woods institutions (the World Bank and the International Monetary Fund) to the United Nations, NATO, the U.S.-Japan Security Treaty, ANZUS (Australia, New Zealand, and United States Treaty), GATT, and the like. The Bush administration and its neoconservative supporters have been very critical of existing international initiatives like the Kyoto Protocol and the International Criminal Court, but have offered up no alternatives in their place that would legitimate and enhance the effectiveness of American action in the world.

3 *Threat, Risk, and Preventive War*

General principles of foreign policy do not dictate what level of risk the United States ought to take to achieve its goals. In pushing for regime change in Iraq, the Bush administration chose a high-risk, high-reward strategy. The risk the administration took was not absurd, especially in light of what was believed about the WMD threat at the time. But it was premised on a very high, specific type of threat, and the administration rolled the dice in a way that required it to be correct simultaneously in several important calculations about future developments. Its self-confidence in its own judgment was misplaced since several of those calculations were questionable even at the time.

The Post–September 11 Threat Environment
It is common for Americans to say that "everything changed after September 11," by which is meant that a new, gravely serious

threat emerged that required a very different set of policy responses. This is certainly correct to a point, and a measure of the change was the fact that the Bush administration could persuade the majority of the American people to support two wars in the Middle East in the eighteen months following the attacks on the twin towers and the Pentagon. It is important to be precise, however, about the ways and degree to which the threat changed, because this influences the kind of risks the United States was justified in running in response.

September 11 changed U.S. threat perceptions because it brought together two threats that were much more deadly in combination than they were separately: radical Islamism and weapons of mass destruction. Both had existed for a long time as issues in U.S. foreign policy, the former since at least the Iranian revolution in 1978 and the latter since the dawn of the nuclear age. Each by itself constituted a serious problem for U.S. foreign policy, but put together in a single package, the two raised for the first time the imminent possibility of a direct, undeterrable nuclear or biological threat to the United States.

The possibility that a relatively small and weak non-state organization could inflict catastrophic damage is something genuinely new in international relations, and it poses an unprecedented security challenge. In most earlier historical periods the ability to inflict serious damage to a society lay only within the purview of states: the entire edifice of international relations theory is built around the presumption that states are the only

significant players in world politics. If catastrophic destruction can be inflicted by non-state actors, then many of the concepts that informed security policy over the past two centuries—
balance of power, deterrence, containment, and the like—lose
their relevance. Deterrence theory in particular depends on the
deployer of any form of WMD having a return address and with
it equities that could be threatened in retaliation.

The real question concerns the likelihood that Islamist terrorists could actually get their hands on a nuclear device, smallpox,
or some other mass casualty–inducing weapon and use it on U.S.
territory. Unfortunately, there is no methodology that allows us
to come to agreement on the scope of this threat. Before September 11, experts on terrorism like Paul Pillar argued that concern with mass-casualty terrorism was overblown and prevented
us from focusing on other, less spectacular threats that were
much more likely. Graham Allison argues, inconsistently, that a
nuclear attack by terrorists is simultaneously "inevitable" and
"preventable." Obviously, it cannot be both; but we are given no
reliable methodology for deciding what the actual level of risk is.
Following the 2001 attacks a large gulf in perceptions between
Americans and Europeans arose over this very issue. Many Americans were convinced that such catastrophic terrorism was both
likely and imminent and that September 11 marked the beginning
of an upward trend in violence. Europeans more often tended
to assimilate the September 11 attacks to their own experience
with terrorism from groups like the Irish Republican Army or

the Basque ETA, regarding it as a surprisingly successful one-of-a-kind event, an outlier in a phenomenon more commonly marked by car bombs or assassinations.[1]

We cannot write off the possibility of a mass-casualty terrorist attack on the United States. There is reason, however, to think that the probability of such an attack has gone down since September 11. The reason is simply that before that date the enormous national security establishment of the United States, as well as the intelligence services and police forces of other countries, were not focused on this issue as a priority. After September 11, they were: though it took a number of months to turn this particular supertanker around and put it on a new course, once there it brought enormous resources to bear against the problem.

How effective those resources are, however, depends on how large the political threat is. If a significant proportion of the world's billion or so Muslims were mobilized to commit suicide terrorism against the United States, then even this security establishment would have difficulties holding back the tide. On the other hand, if the truly dangerous terrorists constituted a relatively small number of people, then the problem would probably be manageable. Part of the threat assessment thus rests on an evaluation of the political dimension of the threat posed by radical Islamists.

Terminology is important. There are significant distinctions between Islamic fundamentalists, Islamists, radical Islamists, and ordinary Muslims, distinctions that became particularly important in the wake of September 11. Islamic fundamentalists act out of religious motives and seek to revive an imagined earlier and purer form of religious practice. Islamists, by contrast, tend to emphasize political goals and want to bring religion into politics in some fashion, though not necessarily in ways that are hostile to democracy. The Islamist Justice and Development Party in Turkey, for example, was democratically elected and has supported Turkish entry into the European Union. Radical Islamists, or jihadists, like Osama bin Laden emphasize the need for violence in pursuit of their political goals. In the following discussion, I shall use *jihadism* to refer to this particular movement.

How serious is the threat posed by Osama bin Laden and jihadists of his ilk to the West, and to our way of life in the United States? Is this an existential threat—that is, a threat capable of undermining the existence of the American regime—on a scale comparable to the threats posed by Nazi Germany or the former Soviet Union? There is a view that says that we are in essence facing "World War IV," having been attacked by an enemy potentially as dangerous and powerful as those we faced in the two world wars and the Cold War. Perhaps the clearest statement of this point of view was offered by Charles Krauthammer:

Disdaining the appeal of radical Islam is the conceit also of secularists. Radical Islam is not just as fanatical and unappeasable in its anti-Americanism, anti-Westernism and anti-modernism as anything we have ever known. It has

the distinct advantage of being grounded in a venerable religion of over one billion adherents that not only provides
a ready supply of recruits—trained and readied in mosques
and *madrassas* far more effective, autonomous and ubiqui-
tous than any Hitler Youth or Komsomol camp—but is
able to draw on a long and deep tradition of zeal, messianic
expectation and a cult of martyrdom. Hitler and Stalin had
to invent these out of whole cloth. Mussolini's version was
a parody. Islamic radicalism flies under a flag with far more
historical depth and enduring appeal than the ersatz reli-
gions of the swastika and hammer-and-sickle that proved
so historically thin and insubstantial. [2]

Krauthammer, in other words, argues that the political threat we
face comes from a version of the religion Islam, that it is thoroughly unappeasable and anti-Western, and that it is deeply and
broadly rooted among the world's more than one billion Muslims.

Each of these assertions is debatable and together vastly overstate the threat that the United States faces in the post–September 11 world. We are not fighting the religion Islam or its adherents but a radical ideology that appeals to a distinct minority of
Muslims. That ideology owes a great deal to Western ideas in addition to Islam, and it appeals to the same alienated individuals
who in earlier generations would have gravitated to communism
or fascism. There is good reason to agree with French Islamic experts Gilles Kepel and Olivier Roy that as a political movement,

jihadism was largely a failure.[3] September 11 and the Iraq war
have given it new life, but the jihadists' ability to seize political
power anywhere is low and has been consistently overestimated
by many in the West. The terrorist threat is real and deadly, but
its most likely form will be isolated attacks in Western Europe or
in Muslim countries, comparable to the Casablanca, Bali, Madrid,
London, and Amman bombings.

Olivier Roy has made a brilliant and persuasive argument that
contemporary jihadism cannot be understood primarily in cultural or religious terms.[4] Genuine Muslim religiosity has always
been embedded in a local or national culture, where the univer-
salist religious doctrine is modified by an accretion of local customs, mores, saints, and the like, and supported by that locale's
political authorities. It is not this type of religiosity that is the
root of present-day terrorism. Islamism and its radical jihadist
offshoots are the product of what Roy calls "deterritorialized"
Islam, in which individual Muslims find themselves cut off from
authentic local traditions, often as uprooted minorities in non-
Muslim lands. This explains why so many jihadists have not come
from the Middle East but have rather been bred (like the September 11 conspirator Mohamed Atta) in Western Europe.

Jihadism is therefore not an attempt to restore a genuine earlier form of Islam but rather an attempt to create a new, universalistic doctrine that can be a source of identity within the context
of the modern, globalized, multicultural world. It is an attempt
to ideologize religion and use it for political purposes, more a

product of modernity (like communism or fascism) than a re-assertion of traditional religion or culture. The historians Ladan and Roya Boroumand have argued similarly that many radical Is-lamist ideas are not Islamic but Western in origin. If we go back through the precursor political thinkers who shaped al-Qaida's ideology, such as Hassan al-Banna and Sayyid Qutb of the Muslim Brotherhood, Maulana Mawdudi of the Jamaat-e-Islami move-ment in Pakistan, or Ayatollah Khomeini, we find a peculiar syncretist doctrine that mixes Islamic ideas with Western ones, borrowed from the extreme left and right of twentieth-century Europe.[5] Concepts like "revolution," "civil society," "state," and the aestheticization of violence come not out of Islam but out of fascism and Marxism-Leninism. Jihadism's purpose is as much political as religious. It is thus a mistake to identify Islamism as an authentic and somehow inevitable expression of Muslim reli-giosity, though it certainly has the power to reinforce religious identity and spark religious hatred.[6]

The implication of this view is that we are not currently en-gaged in anything that looks like a "clash of civilizations" but rather in something that looks much more familiar to us from the experience of the twentieth century. The most dangerous people are not pious Muslims in the Middle East but alienated and uprooted young people in Hamburg, London, or Amster-dam who, like the fascists and Marxists before them, see ideology (in this case, jihadism) as the answer to their personal search for identity. The Madrid bombings of March 11, 2004; the murder of the Dutch filmmaker Theo van Gogh in Amsterdam by Mohammed Bouyeri on November 2, 2004; and the London bombings of July 7, 2005, by a group of British citizens of Pakistani origin all bear this out.

If this interpretation of the nature of the jihadist threat is correct, it has a number of implications for the nature of the struggle ahead. First, the major battlegrounds are as likely to be in Western Europe as in the Middle East. The United States will naturally continue to be a prime terrorist target, but it will not face nearly the same internal threat from its own Muslim residents as many European countries. The United States and its allies will remain engaged in fighting hot wars in Afghanistan and Iraq. But jihadism is a by-product of modernization and globalization, not traditionalism, and hence will be a problem in modern, globalized societies.

In addition, Western democracy will not be a short-term solution to the problem of terrorism. The September 11, Madrid, Amsterdam, and London attackers lived in modern, democratic societies and were not alienated by the lack of democracy in the countries of their birth or ancestry. It was precisely the modern, democratic society they lived in that they found alienating. The long-term problem is thus not one of sealing ourselves off from or somehow "fixing" the Middle East but rather the far more complex one of better integrating people who are already in the West, and doing so in a way that does not undermine the trust and tolerance on which democratic societies are based.

It is also important to recognize the complexity of the cultural background from which jihadism emerges. Simplistic theories that attribute the terrorist problem to religion or culture are not just wrong; they are likely to make the situation worse because they obscure the important fissures that exist within the world of global Islam.

At the center of the terrorist problem is a hard inner core of undeterrable fanatics surrounded by a series of concentric circles representing sympathizers, fellow-travelers, the indifferent, the apolitical, and those sympathetic in differing degrees to the West. The Muslim world is a big, diverse place, and it embraces countries like Mali,[7] Senegal, Turkey, Indonesia, and Malaysia that have all had some success with either democracy or economic modernization. There is considerable evidence that a large number of Muslims in the world, including many living in very traditional Muslim societies, do not hate the United States, modernization, "freedom" (as President Bush would have it), or other aspects of Western civilization. It seems fairly clear that many young Iranians who have grown up under the Islamic dictatorship there do not like it and would much prefer to live in a more open, modern, Western society. A survey undertaken by the U.N. Development Programme across the Arab world showed strong majorities in virtually every Arab state who said that they would like to move to a Western country if they had the opportunity.[8] This suggests they do not find Western culture completely hateful; radicalization is often triggered only later, in second- or third-generation immigrants who have failed to integrate into Western societies.

It is important to separate the technological from the political dimensions of the threat, because this greatly influences what one considers a reasonable response to it and what kinds of risks one is willing to run to meet it. If we are fighting a relatively small number of fanatics sheltering behind a larger group of sympathizers, the conflict begins to look like a counterinsurgency war fought around the globe. This makes an exclusively military response to the challenge inappropriate, since counterinsurgency wars are deeply political and dependent on winning the hearts and minds of the broader population from the beginning.

Poll data indicate that this broader group of Muslims don't dislike the United States or the West as such but rather dislike American foreign policy. They believe that the United States supports Israel one-sidedly against the Palestinians, and supports Arab dictators like Egypt's Mubarak or the Saudi ruling family at the expense of democracy. This is a message that a lot of Americans, and many neoconservatives in particular, have not wanted to hear. Observers like Barry Rubin and Max Boot have argued that when the Arabs say they care about the plight of the Palestinians, they don't actually mean it; criticism of Israel or U.S. support for Israel is a displacement of their unhappiness with their own undemocratic political systems, which they are not able to attack directly.[9]

There is something to the argument that Arab regimes use the Palestinian issue cynically as a means of legitimating themselves and diverting attention from their own failings. And it is true that American peace efforts in the Middle East had no impact on al-Qaida and the jihadists, who were planning the September 11 attacks even as the Oslo Peace Process was in full swing during the Clinton administration. But the seething anger against the United States in the Arab world over Palestine makes it much easier for the hard-core terrorists to operate, providing them with sympathizers, informants, and recruits. (This is not to argue that the United States should abandon Israel to appease their anger, but rather to recognize the fact that that support has costs.) When Arabs say they like the United States but don't like American foreign policy, it would seem both prudent and minimally respectful to take them at their word, rather than putting them on a psychiatrist's couch and telling them that they couldn't possibly mean what they say.

In the long run, today's Islamists may be laying the groundwork for the eventual modernization and transformation of Islamic religious practice. Olivier Roy points out a number of parallels between Islamism and the early years of the Protestant Reformation. Both the Islamists and the early Protestants deracinated religion from the political-cultural matrix within which it was traditionally practiced in favor of a purer, more universalistic form of the religion; both made religion a matter of personal commitment and thus laid the groundwork for modern individualism, where religious identity becomes a lifestyle choice rather than an ascriptive social condition. Many Westerners have lamented the absence of a Muslim Luther. But they forget that the historical Luther did not preach pluralism and liberalism but unleashed a wave of religious fanaticism that played out in very intolerant forms such as those found in the Geneva of John Calvin. It was only by smashing the existing connections between traditional religion and political power, and by exercising actual power in a pluralistic political space, that Protestantism laid the ground-work for modern secular politics and the separation of church and state. In Europe, this process took several centuries; we can only hope for a more accelerated timetable for Muslims today.

A number of large unknowns remain about the nature of the terrorist threat, such as the number of hard-core jihadists, the sources of future supply of new recruits, the locations of the boundaries between the successive rings of potential supporters, and the combination of sticks and carrots that would be neces-sary to separate potential supporters from the inner core of un-deterrables. The Bush administration made a judgment that the appropriate response would be largely stick rather than carrot, and asserted a strong relationship between the new breed of ji-hadists and the old Arab nationalists like Saddam Hussein. These judgments were argued endlessly in the lead-up to and aftermath of the Iraq war.

The Alternative Case for War with Iraq

The Bush administration based its case for war with Iraq on three arguments: first, the fact that Iraq possessed weapons of mass destruction and was in the process of building more; second, that Iraq was linked to al-Qaida and other terrorist organizations; and third, that Iraq was a tyrannical dictatorship from which the Iraqi people deserved to be liberated. This set of arguments was clearly influenced by the September 11 attacks and the new dynamics they established in American politics: by suggesting that Iraqi WMD might end up in the hands of terrorists, the administration sought to build support for military action out of fear that Iraq might directly threaten the American homeland. The administration was thus hoist on its own petard after the war when Iraqi WMD failed to materialize and serious doubts were raised concerning Saddam Hussein's ties to al-Qaida. The administration fell back on the remaining human rights/democracy argument as its principal justification for the war.

There were, however, other less alarmist yet cogent reasons for going to war that the administration could have emphasized that would have left it in a better political position after the war. The first and most important had to do with the untenability of the prewar sanctions regime and the costs it was incurring. Maintenance of no-fly zones over Iraq required a continuing U.S. military presence in Saudi Arabia long after the time that Dick Cheney, as President George H. W. Bush's defense secretary, had promised U.S. forces would be withdrawn. It was the American presence that Osama bin Laden seemed to mind to a much greater extent than support for Israel or other Arab regimes.

Iraq and its sympathizers around the Arab world had been

very successful before the war in arguing that the U.N. sanctions were responsible for killing Iraqi children and had to be lifted for moral reasons. After the war the Oil for Food scandal revealed that Saddam Hussein and his international partners were, in fact, responsible for diverting to themselves money intended to help Iraqi children, but before the war it was impossible to convince anyone of this. It appeared to the administration inevitable that the sanctions regime would fall apart over the coming years and eliminate any remaining barriers to Iraq's WMD programs.

The administration could have made a serious but considerably less alarmist case for why Iraqi nuclear weapons would hurt U.S. interests. By the 1990s it was clear that the global nonproliferation regime, which had succeeded in keeping the number of nuclear weapons states to fewer than ten in the first four decades after Hiroshima, was breaking down. India's nuclear test spawned a response by Pakistan, which in turn fueled new efforts by Iran and North Korea—the other two members of the "axis of evil"— to accelerate their programs. The first Gulf War also acted as a stimulus to find a means of counteracting the overwhelming conventional weapons superiority of the United States. Iran and North Korea received direct support for their nuclear programs from A. Q. Khan, father of the Pakistani bomb. Iraq's possession of a nuclear weapon would cement Iran's commitment to have one as well, and might stimulate new programs in Egypt and Saudi Arabia. A fully nuclearized Middle East added a huge new element of danger to one of the world's most unstable regions. In addition, a nuclear Iraq could deter American intervention should the latter decide to have a second go at invading Kuwait.

Preventing the emergence of a fully nuclearized Middle East is one of those "global public goods" that international relations specialists theorize about. Whereas the United States has an important stake in this outcome because it has interests and allies in the region, there are many other people who would benefit as well, beginning with the people of the Middle East, the Europeans who live close by, and people in other regions of the world where countries were likely to follow suit in a general rush to obtain nuclear weapons.

The Bush administration chose not to use the global public goods rationale for its invasion of Iraq but rather played up the direct threat that Iraq posed to the American homeland. It did so because September 11 presented a new, unforeseen opportunity to convince the American people of the need to take military action against Iraq. The opportunism of this stance hurt the administration after the war, when the incredibility of the direct threat became apparent, and it fueled speculation by those already disinclined to trust the United States that Washington's real motive was oil or Israel.

The National Security Strategy of the United States
The most controversial aspect of the Bush administration's grand strategy concerned the doctrine of preemption that was laid out in the president's West Point speech in June 2002 and in the *Na-*

tional Security Strategy of the United States (NSS) published in September 2002.[10] All administrations are required to produce doctrinal statements of this sort. Most are routine, tedious, and pass into history largely unnoticed; not so with the Bush administration's text.

The *NSS* document is, on the surface, unexceptional. It repeats many of the standard goals of American foreign policy, such as the promotion of free democratic governments around the world and a global system of free trade. Its most notable innovation is to take note of the simple fact outlined above, namely, that non-state terrorists armed with weapons of mass destruction could not be dealt with through the usual tools of containment and deterrence. According to the *NSS*, "The gravest danger our nation faces lies at the crossroads of radicalism and technology. Our enemies have openly declared that they are seeking weapons of mass destruction, and evidence indicates that they are doing so with determination. The United States will not allow these efforts to succeed. . . . And, as a matter of common sense and self-defense, America will act against such emerging threats before they are fully formed."[11] The *NSS* argued further that the United States would like to work with traditional alliances and international institutions wherever possible, but that if it could not get international agreement over defending itself from potentially catastrophic terrorism, it would need to resort to "coalitions of the willing."

Neither preemption nor unilateralism was a new feature of American foreign policy. John Lewis Gaddis has shown that preemption (often unilateral preemption) has been used by American administrations since the early nineteenth century; it was seriously considered at several points during the Cold War.[12] The Eisenhower administration debated a preemptive "rollback" strategy in the early 1950s, and the Kennedy administration considered preempting the Soviet medium-range missiles deployed to Cuba during the Cuban Missile Crisis.

What was revolutionary about the *NSS* was its expansion of traditional notions of preemption to include what amounted to preventive war. Preemption is usually understood to be an effort to break up an imminent military attack; preventive war is a military operation designed to head off a threat that is months or years away from materializing. The Bush administration argued that in an age of nuclear-armed terrorists, the very distinction between preemption and prevention was outmoded; the restrictive definition of the former needed to be broadened.[13] The United States would periodically find it necessary to reach inside states and create political conditions that would prevent terrorism. It thereby rejected Westphalian notions of the need to respect state sovereignty and work with existing governments, tacitly accepting both the neoconservatives' premise about the importance of regimes and the justifications for the humanitarian interventions undertaken during the 1990s.

Problems

The view that states can legitimately preempt *imminent* threats was endorsed after the Iraq war by the U.N. High Level Panel.[14] *If* a country is clearly faced with a catastrophic threat from a non-state actor or a rogue state, and *if* it is unable to get help from existing international institutions to meet that threat, it can legitimately take matters into its own hands and move preemptively to break up that threat.

The problem with the *NSS* doctrine was that in order to justify stretching the definition of preemption to include preventive war against nonimminent threats, the administration needed to be right about the dangers facing the United States. As it turned out, it overestimated the threat from Iraq specifically, and from nuclear terrorism more generally. Furthermore, the administration conflated the threat of nuclear terrorism with the rogue state/proliferation problem, and applied the preventive war remedy to the lesser of the two dangers.

The actual experience of the Iraq war ought to demonstrate that the distinction between preemptive and preventive war remains a significant one. We have not abruptly moved into a world in which rogue states routinely pass WMD to terrorists; such a world may yet emerge, but acting as if it were here now forces us into some extremely costly choices. Even under post–September 11 conditions, preventive war remains far more difficult to justify prudentially and morally than preemptive war and ought properly to be used in a far more restricted number of cases.

There are certainly historical instances in which preventive war might retrospectively have saved the world a great deal of misery. The classic case cited by many was Hitler's remilitarization of the Rhineland in 1936, a clear violation of Germany's post–World War I obligations, undertaken at a time when Britain and France collectively had an overwhelming military advantage over Germany. By waiting to declare war on Germany until after the Sudetenland crisis in 1938, Britain and France allowed Germany to rearm to the point where it could invade Poland and defeat France. Israel's destruction of Iraq's Osirak reactor in 1981 was widely seen as a successful application of preventive war, insofar as it set the Iraqi nuclear weapons program back by several years; when Saddam Hussein invaded Kuwait ten years later he didn't have a bomb. [15]

One of the reasons why preventive war has always been regarded as prudentially problematic, however, is that it depends on being able to accurately predict the future. We know in retrospect what people in 1936 did not fully understand—namely, that Hitler would go on to dismember Czechoslovakia and plan a war against Poland. Perhaps they should have known and were being criminally naive, but that is a judgment easier to make after the fact. British Prime Minister Anthony Eden in 1956 believed he was in a Rhineland-type situation when he went ahead with the Suez war, failing to foresee that Egypt's President Nasser would not ultimately present the same threat to world security as Hitler. The Germans in the first decade of the twentieth century feared the weakest member of the Concert of Europe, Russia, based on projections of Russian power out into the future and prepared for war against the country before it became too strong. It is perhaps not surprising that the great German Chancellor Otto von Bismarck labeled preventive war "committing suicide for fear of death."[16]

Ken Jowitt puts the problem in the following terms:

So the logic behind an anticipatory strategy is powerful. However, its strategic application demands the combined wisdom of Pericles and Solomon. To begin with, the premise for an anticipatory attack posits a hostile leader and regime platonically impervious to any environmental changes whether domestic or international. This is not always a mistaken premise—Hitler and Pol Pot are cases in point— but it is *almost* always mistaken. Over time, most regimes do change substantially if not essentially. One has only to look at the Soviet Union after 1956 and China after 1978.

An anticipatory strategy also relies on American presidential administrations with an unerring ability to identify which leaders and regimes are impervious to environmental changes. Any mistake in identification would result not in preemption or anticipation, but in a war that could have been avoided.[17]

Some people argue that Solomonic wisdom could be had if only we had better intelligence. Better information about our enemies' future plans would always be welcome, but it is foolish to think that bigger intelligence budgets or reorganizations of the intelligence community would produce substantially more accurate predictions about the future.

The problem with intelligence, as Roberta Wohlstetter demonstrated many years ago, lies not in inadequate information but rather in the signal-to-noise ratio of that information.[18] Most proposed intelligence community reforms will increase the volume of both signals *and* noise, rather than increasing the ratio of the former to the latter. The ability to pick out signals will continue to depend on cognitive factors like prior expectations, mental frameworks, incentives, and the like that we will never get completely right. The intelligence community had every incentive to overestimate the Iraqi WMD threat in 2003 because it had underestimated the threat in 1991 and did not want to be fooled again. There is no set of intelligence reforms that will fix this kind of problem or allow us to accurately predict the future.

Given these uncertainties, it is easy to see why preventive war, as opposed to preemption, has not been used frequently as an instrument of state power. Obviously, preventive war is more justifiable the nearer the threat is; a nuclear program on the verge of testing or weaponization is a better candidate for prevention than one that is still in the planning stages. If we had evidence that other rogue or failed states beyond Afghanistan were harboring nuclear-armed terrorists, then the preemption/prevention distinction would indeed collapse. Preventive strikes would have to be at least considered if Pakistan, with its nuclear weapons, fell into chaos or was taken over by radical Islamists at some future date. Thus preventive war cannot be ruled out as a component of an American grand strategy. But making it a central feature entails large risks and costs that are all too evident in retrospect.

The second problem with the Bush administration's approach to preemption as outlined in the *NSS* was its failure to distinguish between preemptive/preventive war designed to stop catastrophic terrorism and the use of the same policy as a means of stopping proliferation by rogue states. As indicated above, acquisition of nuclear weapons by rogue states is a serious problem that deserves a strong response by the international community, but it is of a considerably lower order of magnitude than the possibility of a rogue state giving a bomb to a terrorist organization for use against the United States. President Bush and other members of the administration stated clearly that their preventive war policy was being driven by the latter consideration, as when he said in a speech before the war that Americans could not wait for "the smoking gun—that could come in the form of a mushroom cloud."[19]

Before the war, there was insufficient discussion of the proposition that rogue state proliferators, including Iraq, would be willing to donate or sell their nuclear weapons to terrorist groups. Those making the case for such a likelihood proffered two arguments. The first was that Iraq had already supported terrorists in the 1993 attempt to blow up the World Trade Center using a truck bomb, and Saddam Hussein had subsequently maintained links with al-Qaida. The second argument, made by Kenneth Pollack in his influential book *The Threatening Storm* (2002), was that Saddam Hussein was not a rational actor and was therefore not deterrable.[20]

The argument that there were ties between Saddam Hussein and al-Qaida was extensively debated within the intelligence community before the war, and much more publicly after it. Although there was circumstantial evidence linking Iraqi intelligence to the 1993 attack, the connection could not ultimately be verified, as was the case with later contacts like the alleged meeting between September 11 hijacker Mohamed Atta and an Iraqi intelligence agent in Prague.[21] The mere existence of contacts does not, of course, prove that there was substantive collaboration between Iraq and al-Qaida, that Iraq planned the September 11 attacks, or that Iraq would donate WMD to al-Qaida. Indeed, the Bush administration eventually stated for the record that there was no evidence linking Iraq to September 11.

The more important question concerns likely behavior and the issue of Saddam Hussein's rationality raised by the Pollack book. The problem with the latter case is that rationality is not a binary condition, whereby a leader is either rational and deterrable or irrational and undeterrable. Saddam Hussein's record, as described by Pollack, shows him to be both a risk-taker and someone with very poor judgment (as opposed, say, to an equally brutal but much more prudent dictator like Hafiz Assad of

Syria). But Saddam Hussein is not someone who was inclined to take on the role of a suicide bomber and risk nuclear retaliation for attacking America, nor does it seem plausible that he would go to the trouble of building a bomb only to give it away to a group he did not control.

If Iraq's giving nuclear weapons to suicide terrorists was implausible, the real debate ought to have been about the merits of waging preventive war to prevent a rogue but ultimately deterrable state from getting nuclear weapons. This concern, as noted above, was an utterly serious one, but the stakes would have been lower and the threshold for intervention consequently higher.

Indeed, the broader question that should have been raised then and that should be discussed now is whether preventive war ought to be a key instrument in dealing with nuclear proliferation now that the earlier restraints posed by the Nonproliferation Treaty regime have broken down. There are several reasons for thinking that preventive war is no longer a good option.

First, it has become over time increasingly difficult in operational terms to preemptively destroy budding nuclear programs. The very success of the Israeli strike against Osirak has meant that a similar strike in the future would be much more difficult as proliferating states move their facilities underground or harden or disperse them. The miserable failure of American intelligence to accurately identify WMD capabilities in Iraq, and its inability to assess the truth of current North Korean claims to have a bomb, suggest the difficulties that will face future preemptive strikes.[22]

The second problem is that while preemption or the threat of preemption may indeed deter proliferation (as some have argued was the case with Libya), it could in other cases serve as a stimulus to proliferation. Neither North Korea nor Iran seems to have concluded that it must give up its nuclear weapons program and disarm as a result of the Iraq war; Pyongyang, indeed, appears to have accelerated the North Korean program with the idea that possession of a nuclear weapon would be a strong deterrent to U.S. attack. Preemption in any event only slows, but does not stop, proliferation.

The third problem is that if the United States seeks to use not just precision air strikes but regime change as a means of stopping rogue state proliferators, it has to be able to manage the process of regime change successfully. The American experience in Iraq has now probably scotched the kind of casual talk that could be heard before the war about planning to "take down" Pakistan—a country with eight times the population of Iraq—in the event it was taken over by radical Islamists.

Finally, the value of the delay gained by using military force to stop proliferation needs to be weighed against the political damage that such action might entail. This dilemma is evident in Iran today: a significant part of the Iranian population opposes the regime of the mullahs in Teheran and is well disposed toward the

United States. But part of this opposition is also quite nationalistic and might actually favor a more liberal Iran that possessed nuclear weapons. An American military strike at Iranian facilities would probably undercut this opposition and set back prospects for internal reform.

Justified Risk?

All foreign policies, including doing nothing and maintaining the status quo, involve risks. The proper way to assess the Bush administration's handling of foreign policy in the aftermath of September 11 is not to ask whether it took risks but whether those risks were reasonable based on information available at the time the decision was made.

In retrospect, the danger represented by Saddam Hussein's regime was evidently much lower than portrayed by the administration. Not only did he apparently not have an ongoing nuclear weapons program, he did not possess the considerable stocks of biological and chemical weapons asserted by Secretary of State Colin Powell in his February 6, 2003, speech to the U.N. Security Council. The sanctions regime of the 1990s had apparently been sufficient to convince Saddam to get rid of his residual weapons; the administration's skepticism about the effectiveness of inspections was misplaced. In light of the reports of the Iraq Survey Group (ISG) headed first by David Kay and then by Charles Duelfer, Saddam Hussein had the intention of pursuing a program to acquire WMD capabilities once sanctions were lifted, but this put the imminent threat postulated by the administration much further off into the future.[23]

The U.S. intelligence community, the U.N. weapons inspectors, and most non-U.S. intelligence services believed that Iraq had limited hidden stocks of chemical and biological weapons, and virtually everyone was astonished when the ISG came up empty-handed. It is therefore hard to blame the Bush administration for believing that these stockpiles existed.

On the other hand, evidence that Iraq had restarted its nuclear program, as Vice President Cheney once asserted, was not there, and the administration was clearly guilty of greatly exaggerating this particularly frightening aspect of the threat. In addition, by referring to WMD generically and not separating nuclear from chemical and biological weapons, the administration implied that the nuclear threat was much greater than it was.

Although many people would today like to believe that the Iraq war was from the start a criminal conspiracy based on outright fabrications, it is more likely that administration officials were guilty of exaggerating rather than lying, if by lying is meant deliberately stating something that one knows to be false. They believed that Saddam Hussein was trying to get nuclear weapons and that if the evidence were not as clear as they would have liked, it would eventually materialize and vindicate their point of view. Their deeper fault was to not have any self-doubts or to engage in a more open-minded review of the evidence before launching a preventive war.

After the Iraq Survey Group reported its failure to find WMD in Iraq, President Bush continued to assert that preventive war was justified because the ISG found that the Iraqi regime had had the *intention* of acquiring WMD at some point in the future. If the simple positing of an intention to acquire WMD (as opposed to evidence of stockpiles or ongoing production program) is sufficient to trigger a preventive war, many countries in the world qualify as potential targets of U.S. intervention. I doubt that the president had in mind this kind of stretching of the criterion for preventive war; the outcome of the Iraqi WMD imbroglio suggests, however, that the doctrine as a whole needs to be revisited and revised.

4 *American Exceptionalism and International Legitimacy*

Many neoconservatives argued during the late 1990s that the United States should use its military predominance to assert "benevolent hegemony" over strategically important parts of the world. By invading Iraq, the Bush administration saw itself not as acting out of narrow self-interest but as providing a global public good. The administration's belief in its own good motives explains much of its failure to anticipate the highly negative international reaction to the war.

Many people have asserted that the Bush administration was contemptuous of international public opinion and the legitimacy that multilateral institutions are said to confer. It is true that many members of the administration had a low opinion of the United Nations, as exemplified by State Department Undersecretary and future U.N. Ambassador John Bolton. But dislike of the United Nations is not necessarily the same thing as contempt for international legitimacy. Many members of the Bush administration believed that the experience of the Cold War, the first Gulf War, and the Balkans showed that legitimacy is sometimes rewarded by the international system ex post rather than ex ante, and that owing to weaknesses of the collective decision-making institutions in world politics, the United States would have to act first and receive approbation later.[1] This was a background condition that explained (but did not necessarily justify) the administration's seemingly contemptuous treatment of its European allies.

There was another argument made by many members of the administration, namely, that the United States already had international legal sanction—and thus the legitimate right—to invade Iraq because in doing so it was merely enforcing the previous seventeen U.N. resolutions mandating Iraq's disarmament.[2] It is certainly true that Saddam Hussein acted in violation of many U.N. resolutions, particularly when he expelled the United Nations Special Commission (UNSCOM) inspectors from Iraq in 1999. As became painfully evident after the war, Iraq flagrantly misused the money from the United Nation's Oil for Food program and constantly tested the limits of the post–Gulf War ceasefire.

Although this record is clear, what is less clear was the legal right under international law of two permanent members of the U.N. Security Council, the United States and Britain, to enforce

U.N. resolutions on their own. The United Nations has no executive branch charged with enforcing its decisions, and a strong case can be made that delegation of enforcement powers to specific countries requires a separate decision and vote. The United Nations, in any event, cannot legally bind itself in perpetuity or prevent its members from changing their minds. It is true that the U.N. Security Council did not vote to rescind any of the resolutions that Iraq was guilty of violating; on the other hand, it was clear on the eve of the Iraq war that the majority of its members did not want the United States and Britain to unilaterally enforce its edicts. In any event, the Bush administration had made it fairly clear at that point that the United States would not feel itself bound by what the Security Council did, making its own conformity with international law selective and therefore suspect in the eyes of many.

Ultimately, the international legitimacy of American actions was not a legal but a political matter. On the eve of the war, it was clear that the vast majority of public opinion around the world opposed the American invasion, including majorities in countries officially supporting the United States like Britain, Spain, and Italy. This in the end would not have mattered if the United States had been able to demonstrate ex post the logic and necessity of the intervention—for example by uncovering a vigorous underground nuclear weapons program. After all, it is precisely this type of political legitimacy that the United States has sought and won in earlier crises, and the administration was right to criticize its opponents for overemphasizing international law as the sole basis for legitimate action.

The collective action problem perceived by many in the Bush administration lay with the United Nations and with the Europeans who wanted to work through it to solve serious security threats requiring military intervention. The Clinton administration's experience in the Balkans convinced many in the Bush administration that the United Nations was incapable of solving serious security challenges. In Bosnia, a U.N.-mandated arms embargo and the pretense of impartiality actually ended up benefiting the party clearly at the root of the problem, Serbia. The restricted rules of engagement used by the European-led U.N. peacekeeping force resulted in the spectacle of Dutch peacekeepers in Srebrenica, unable to defend themselves much less the Bosnians they were charged to protect, being taken hostage by the Serbs. Similarly, in the Kosovo crisis the Russian veto prevented the Security Council from acting at all. The United States in the mid-1990s would have been perfectly happy to let the Europeans handle a problem that was, after all, in their own backyard. But both the Bosnia and Kosovo crises were resolved only when the United States entered the picture and used its military power in a decisive way. The United States brokered the Dayton Accords that brought the Bosnian conflict to a close and led the military coalition that stopped Serbian aggression in Kosovo, ultimately paving the way for regime change in Belgrade.

Defense Secretary Donald Rumsfeld took a particularly jaundiced view of Europe's ability to act. It is not clear whether he was enthusiastic from the start about the need for American intervention in the Balkans, and he believed that the United States had become bogged down there because the Clinton administration's desire to work through multilateral institutions like NATO tied its hands. General Wesley Clark, the NATO commander who led the intervention in Kosovo and later ran for president as a Democrat, recounts running into a senior member of the Bush administration after the 2000 election who told him, "We read your book—no one is going to tell us where we can or can't bomb."[3]

What happened in the Balkans during the 1990s was only the latest iteration of a pattern of behavior that has been labeled by Stephen Sestanovich American Maximalism.[4] It is a pattern that was established at the beginning of the Cold War, wherein Americans consistently pushed for goals that were more ambitious and outside the boundaries of conventional thinking than those of their European allies. European indecisiveness and inability to create robust decision-making institutions meant that the United States frequently had to step in to force important issues on the agenda. This was true in the case of deployment of medium-range missiles in the 1980s, in the Reagan administration's subsequent proposal to remove them entirely through a double-zero option, and in American pressure for a Europe "whole and free" in 1989.

Mancur Olsen, in *The Logic of Collective Action* (1965), notes that public goods are often supplied unilaterally by a single actor who is much stronger than the others and permits free-riding by the other players because that actor has a powerful interest in securing those goods.[5] Many people have argued that this was the situation of the United States vis-à-vis its allies both in Europe and in Asia during the Cold War, and it produced a unilateralist mindset on the part of members of the Bush administration going into the Iraq war. The administration made less of a break from earlier patterns of U.S. foreign policy than many have suggested.

The Bush administration and its neoconservative supporters failed to anticipate the hostility of the global reaction to the war before undertaking it, particularly in Europe. The administration had made a tactical error in failing to foresee that French president Jacques Chirac and his foreign minister Dominique de Villepin would double-cross Colin Powell by withdrawing support for the second U.N. Security Council resolution on the war. But opposition to the war was not a matter of elites and their political calculations. On February 15, 2003, a month before the start of war, massive antiwar demonstrations took place all over Europe, including London, Madrid, and Rome, capitals of the three European allies that had agreed to join the Bush administration's "coalition of the willing." Indeed, Europe had never before appeared as spontaneously unified around a single issue as this one, which is why former French finance minister Dominique Strauss-Kahn labeled the demonstrations the "birth of the European nation."[6] There are many reasons for thinking that, unlike earlier trans-Atlantic spats, the rift caused by the Iraq war was in the nature of a tectonic shift, a rift that will not easily be healed in the future.

The reasons why the Iraq war provoked such an upsurge of anti-Americanism are complex and will be explored at greater length below. But there was a short-term reason for this resistance that was built into the *National Security Strategy* doctrine of preventive war: its implicit recognition of American exceptionalism. Clearly, a doctrine of preventive war is not one that can be safely generalized throughout the international system. Many countries face terrorist threats and might be inclined to deal with them through preemptive intervention or the overturning of regimes deemed to harbor terrorists. Russia, China, and India all fall into this category, yet if any of them announced a general strategy of preemptive/preventive war as a means of dealing with terrorism, the United States would doubtless be the first country to object. The fact that the United States granted itself a right that it would deny to other countries is based, in the *NSS*, on an implicit judgment that the United States is different from other countries and can be trusted to use its military power justly and wisely in ways that other powers could not.

This line of thinking has a long history in the way that Americans think about themselves. It starts with Washington's Farewell Address and the notion that the American republic was born in virtue and would only be contaminated if it were to play the kinds of power-political games practiced by the Europeans.

What was only implicit in the Bush administration's official policy pronouncements had been stated explicitly by a number of neoconservative writers in the years leading up to the Iraq war. One of the earliest assertions about the need for America to exert hegemonic power to achieve global order and security came from Charles Krauthammer, who argued at the end of the Cold War that the United States faced a "unipolar moment," when no other power existed to challenge American hegemony. Krauthammer elsewhere argued that the United States does not, like other great powers, seek empire, but rather will act as "custodian of the international system."[7]

Similarly, William Kristol and Robert Kagan, writing about American foreign policy in the late 1990s in their book *Present Dangers*, argued explicitly in favor of a policy of benevolent hegemony in which the United States would use its power to create a benign, peaceful, and democratic world order. They speculated specifically on the question of whether such hegemony would engender opposition and resistance, but concluded that it would not because of America's unusual degree of virtue: "But the unwillingness of other powers to gang up on the United States also has something to do with the fact that it does not pursue a narrow, selfish definition of its national interest, but generally finds its interests in a benevolent international order. In other words, it is precisely *because American foreign policy is infused with an unusually high degree of morality* that other nations find they have less to fear from its otherwise daunting power" (italics added).[8] It is hard to read these lines unironically in the wake of the global reaction to the Iraq war. It is not sufficient that Americans believe in their own good intentions; non-Americans must be convinced of them as well.

The idea that the United States has in the past acted in a broad-minded way and that it has provided global public goods has considerable plausibility. The post–World War II transformations of Germany and Japan into democracies and allies, America's support for the Bretton Woods institutions and the United Nations in the 1940s, and the support given to Western Europe through the Marshall Plan and to the "captive nations" of Eastern Europe during the Cold War provided broad public benefits to the global community even as they suited American strategic interests. The United States could easily have opted for isolationism instead, as many Americans argued up through the late 1940s, and might well have been less generous in its sustenance of allies throughout this period.

By the time of the Iraq war, however, the idea that non-Americans would react favorably or at least acquiesce in an American assertion of benevolent hegemony was more a hope than a fact. Before other countries accepted U.S. leadership, they would have to be convinced not just that America was good but that it was also wise in its application of power, and, through that wisdom, successful in achieving the ends it set for itself. The violently negative feelings that emerged after the war had their roots in developments that preceded the Bush administration, signs of which could and should have been picked up in the years preceding.

The problems with the *National Security Strategy of the United States* weren't limited to the concept of preemption contained in the document, or to its assertion that the United States might occasionally need to act through coalitions of the willing. Also problematic was that the strategy did not lay out any criteria for deciding when the United States would undertake a preventive war. National Security Advisor Condoleezza Rice did state shortly after the *NSS* was published that "this approach must be treated with great caution. The number of cases in which it might be justified will always be small. It does not give a green light—to the United States or any other nation—to act first without exhausting other means, including diplomacy. Preemptive action does not come at the beginning of a long chain of effort. The threat must be very grave. And the risks of waiting must far outweigh the risks of action."[9]

This message should have been embedded within the *NSS* itself, along with more specific criteria outlining conditions under which preemption might legitimately be used. It then needed to be repeated incessantly as the administration made its case for action against Iraq. What happened instead was that a much more diffuse message was presented, suggesting a broader application of the preemption doctrine. President Bush in his 2002 state of the union address had talked about an "axis of evil" consisting of Iraq, Iran, and North Korea, and it was only natural that foreign observers would put this phrase together with the new preemption doctrine and assume that the administration was planning a series of three preventive wars.

There are several possible explanations for why so experienced a foreign policy team made such elementary blunders. The first was a confusion of audiences. Much of the Bush administration's tough talk was aimed at the rogue states themselves and other actors that might be inclined to support them. Bush's famous post–September 11 line about being "for us or against us" in the war on terrorism was doubtless aimed at countries like Pakistan or Yemen that had in the past harbored terrorists and were in the process of deciding whether to cooperate with the United States in hunting down al-Qaida operatives. The problem was that the phrase was heard in Europe as a challenge to get with the Bush administration's agenda in a take-it-or-leave-it fashion, which they naturally resented. The administration, unfortunately, did little to clarify the question of which audience was being addressed.

A second reason for this communications failure may have had to do with the fact that there was still disagreement within the administration over the conditions under which the doctrine would be applied, a disagreement that prevented anyone from laying them out explicitly. Some in the Department of Defense may indeed have wanted to keep the door open to multiple preventive wars and hence were not willing to acknowledge any public diplomacy guidance that would have limited U.S. options.

Finally, Colin Powell did not see speech-making and doctrinal pronouncements as central to his job as secretary of state. He told close associates that he felt uncomfortable with big ideas and abstract doctrines. It has frequently been remarked that Powell did less speaking and traveling than most of his predecessors; in the critical period between the votes on the first and second U.N. Security Council resolutions authorizing the war, for example, he remained mostly in Washington. In fairness to him, he may have felt that he did not have the authority to say the sorts of things to U.S. allies that would have allayed their fears about the United States embarking on an open-ended series of preventive wars.

There was a broad failure on the part of American elites to perceive an underlying trend of anti-Americanism—what Walter Russell Mead calls "the growing storm"—in the period between the end of the Cold War and the outbreak of the Iraq war.[10] Americans had grown used to being disliked during the Cold War, and it was easy to write off new manifestations of anti-American feeling as a recrudescence of a familiar left-wing hostility to U.S. power and purposes.

But something different was brewing this time. The level of extreme hostility in the Middle East and the Muslim world reached unprecedented levels in the period following September 11, with positive feelings about the United States falling to 5 percent in Jordan, 21 percent in Pakistan, 27 percent in Morocco, and 30 percent in Turkey—all traditional friends.[11] A milder unhappiness was shared among America's closest friends and allies, countries with whom Americans thought they shared common values and who had been the primary beneficiaries when the United States opposed Nazi Germany and the former Soviet Union. In Western Europe, moreover, criticism came not just from the usual suspects on the left but from many in the center and on the right who had anchored American influence during the Cold War.

Part of the explanation for this phenomenon lies in the shift that took place from the 1980s onward toward what Mead calls "millennial capitalism." Up until the conservative Reagan and Thatcher revolutions, all industrialized countries including the United States had built generous welfare states with growing entitlements and extensive government management of market competition. This system was moving rapidly toward a crisis of overregulation and falling productivity growth by the late 1970s. The United States led the way in the reversal of this trend, partially dismantling its postwar welfare state. American markets had always been less regulated than their European counterparts, and the difference became even more conspicuous in the last two decades of the twentieth century as the United States deregulated airlines, telecommunications, electricity, and other services. This unleashed a wave of technological innovation and growth that was associated with the information technology boom of the 1990s.

Americans are justly proud of their role in inventing the transistor, the integrated circuit, the personal computer, and the Internet. Many feel that these developments could have emerged only in a freewheeling, competitive capitalist order with minimal government interference in private markets. There is a distinctively American form of techno-libertarianism that translates traditional American antistatism into a modern high-tech setting, exemplified by John Perry Barlow and the Electronic Frontier Foundation that he helped found.[12]

The view that the American information technology industry owed its success to the absence of government intervention is only partially correct. Most of the major American technological advances of the late twentieth century were stimulated by government encouragement and investment.[13] But there was enough truth in the techno-libertarian view to convince many Americans that their particular mix of market and state represented the wave of the future. Conversely, Europe came to be regarded as overregulated, retrograde, and antimarket.

The wave of newly invigorated capitalist competition that was unleashed in the 1990s came to be debated under the heading of "globalization" and was regarded in much of the world with a mixture of fascination, envy, fear, and resentment. There were, of course, countries like South Korea, Taiwan, and China that took full advantage of globalization to open up export markets and grow. But the other industrialized democracies were comfortable with their welfare states and often saw the American drive to liberalize markets around the world not as a well-intentioned effort to promote reform but as an American attempt to impose its own antistatist values on the rest of the world in a "race to the bottom."

Much of the drive to Americanize the global economy came out of the private sector and the challenge posed by newly competitive U.S. companies and financial institutions. But American government policy was highly supportive of economic liberalization as well, in ways that generated a backlash that often went unperceived in Washington. The Washington Consensus was a package of orthodox economic liberalization measures that were often attached as conditions to structural adjustment lending packages by international financial institutions like the International Monetary Fund (IMF) and the World Bank for developing countries.[14] Had this type of U.S.-promoted economic liberalization produced consistently positive results, there might have been greater acceptance of this form of benevolent hegemony. But even countries like Argentina that thought they were following American advice found themselves in serious economic crisis by the end of the 1990s. The result was a general discrediting of "neoliberalism" across Latin America and the rise of a new generation of leftist leaders in the region.[15]

In places like Thailand and South Korea, the Clinton administration pushed strongly for capital market liberalization during the first half of the 1990s. Those promoting these policies, like Treasury secretary Robert Rubin and his deputy, Larry Summers (later his successor), saw this simply as a matter of good policy that would benefit the countries in question. Many Asians, on the other hand, looked at U.S. motives more suspiciously, seeing this as an effort to force open closed capital markets on behalf of Wall Street, where Rubin, a former head of Goldman Sachs, not coincidentally had many friends.

When the Asian crisis of 1997–98 hit, these same countries were devastated by the outrush of liquidity that capital market liberalization had fostered. Most observers now agree that capital account liberalization had been undertaken prematurely, before regulatory systems were in place that would have fortified these economies against the vagaries of international capital markets. Moreover, the IMF's first instinct was to apply the medicine of fiscal austerity to countries that, if anything, needed more public spending. Yet despite its responsibility for at least some of the conditions that led to the crisis, the United States did not come to Thailand's aid, and it used its influence over international institutions like the IMF to force further capital market liberalization when the target countries were economically prostrate. It is no wonder that the Koreans to this day refer to the crisis as the "IMF crisis" rather than a crisis of their own policies and institutions.

In the political sphere, American hegemony had certain unanticipated negative effects. The Cold War had forced the United States to pay attention to many parts of the world where it did not otherwise have strong direct economic or political interests. That attention often came in the form of military aid or intervention, with problematic consequences for the country in question. But after the end of the Cold War, the United States often felt free to disengage entirely from these countries.[16] Afghanistan was the classic example, and it came back to haunt Washington after September 11. Lack of Soviet competition freed the United States to support democratic movements in places like the Philippines and Chile where it had earlier bolstered authoritarian rulers, but the United States was also freed to look the other way when terrible things happened in places like Rwanda and Liberia.

The notion that the American Cold War leadership role could be transformed into a posture of benevolent hegemony vis-à-vis the rest of the world contains within it a number of structural flaws and contradictions that make it untenable as a long-term basis for conceptualizing American foreign policy.

First, benevolent hegemony rests on a belief in American exceptionalism that most non-Americans simply find not credible. The idea that the United States behaves disinterestedly on the world stage is not widely believed because it is for the most part not true and, indeed, could not be true if American leaders fulfill their responsibilities to the American people. The United States is capable of acting generously in its provision of global public goods, and has been most generous when its ideals and self-interests have coincided. But the United States is also a great power with interests not related to global public goods. American presidents have to protect the often narrow economic interests of particular constituents; they have to worry about the security of energy supplies; they have to respond to the demands of various ethnic constituencies within the United States; and they need cooperation from a variety of countries regardless of how those countries treat their own citizens. There are plenty of global public goods, from African peacekeeping to abating carbon emissions, that the United States finds too burdensome to provide.

The second problem with benevolent hegemony is that it presupposes an extremely high level of competence on the part of the hegemonic power. Many critics of the Bush administration in Europe and the Middle East before the Iraq war did not question the war on abstract normative grounds (that is, that it was not blessed by a second U.N. Security Council resolution). Rather, they wondered whether the administration really understood what was involved in the political transformation of the Middle East that it was undertaking. In these concerns, they were quite prescient.

The final problem with benevolent hegemony lies in domestic American politics. There are sharp limits to the American people's attention to foreign affairs and willingness to fund projects overseas that do not have clear benefits to U.S. interests. September 11 changed that calculus in many ways, providing popular support for two wars in the Middle East and large increases in defense spending. But the durability of the support is uncertain: although most Americans want to do what is necessary to make the project of rebuilding Iraq succeed, the aftermath of the war did not increase public appetite for further costly interventions. A deeper problem lies in the fact that Americans are not, at heart, an imperial people. Even benevolent hegemons sometimes have to act ruthlessly, and they need a staying power that does not come easily to people who are reasonably content with their own lives and society.

5 *Social Engineering and the Problem of Development*

It is in the area of political and economic development that two important neoconservative principles potentially collide. On the one hand, neoconservatives rightly believe that the internal character of a regime is important: liberal democracies tend to respect the basic human rights of their citizens and are less externally aggressive than dictatorships. So there is an imperative to liberate people from tyranny and promote democracy around the world by reaching inside states and shaping their basic institutions. This stands in sharp contrast to realist foreign policy, which tends to respect sovereignty and be indifferent to the internal character of other states.

On the other hand, another strand of neoconservative thought has emphasized the dangers of overly ambitious social engineering. This is a theme that goes all the way back to the original anti-Stalinism of the City College crowd and extends through the writers in *The Public Interest* who criticized American social programs for bringing about unintended consequences that undermined their original purposes. As noted earlier, a major theme running through James Q. Wilson's extensive writings on crime was the idea that one could not lower crime rates by trying to solve deep underlying problems like poverty and racism; effective policies needed to focus on shorter-term measures that went after symptoms rather than root causes. Translated into the domain of foreign policy, this principle should have induced caution in expectations for the kind of political transformation that would be possible in the Middle East by, for example, promoting democracy.[1]

Neither the Bush administration nor its neoconservative supporters gave adequate thought before the Iraq war to how this conundrum could be resolved. Though loath to admit it after the fact, the administration vastly underestimated the cost and difficulty of reconstructing Iraq and guiding it toward a democratic transition. In its internal prewar planning, the Pentagon evidently estimated that it could draw its forces down from the initial 150,000 to only 60,000 troops some six months after the end of active combat. In an interview on the eve of the war, Vice President Cheney gave an interview to Tim Russert in which he said that "to suggest that we need several hundred thousand troops there after military operations cease, after the conflict ends, I don't think is accurate. . . . I really do believe we will be greeted as liberators."[2] President Bush would not have landed on an aircraft carrier bearing a "Mission Accomplished" banner had he known that nearly 150,000 U.S. soldiers would still be fighting a vicious counterinsurgency war two years later.

There was a tendency among promoters of the war to believe that democracy was a default condition to which societies would revert once liberated from dictators. In a speech to the American Enterprise Institute given on the eve of the war, the president said: "Human cultures can be vastly different. Yet the human heart desires the same good things, everywhere on Earth. In our desire to be safe from brutal and bullying oppression, human beings are the same. In our desire to care for our children and give them a better life, we are the same. For these fundamental reasons, freedom and democracy will always and everywhere have greater appeal than the slogans of hatred and the tactics of terror." One can argue that there is a universal human desire to be free of tyranny and a universalism to the appeal of life in a prosperous liberal democracy. The problem is one of the time frame involved. It is one thing to say that there is a broad, centuries-long trend toward the spread of liberal democracy—something that I myself have strongly argued in the past—and another to say that either democracy or prosperity can emerge in a given society at a given time.[3] There are certain critical intervening variables known as *institutions* that must be in place before a society can move from an amorphous longing for freedom to a well-functioning, consolidated democratic political system with a modern economy. And if there is one thing that the study of democratic transitions and political development teaches, it is that institutions are very difficult to establish.

The 1990s saw tremendous intellectual ferment on the question of institutional development; there is today a huge academic- and practitioner-based literature on democratic transitions, and an even larger literature on institutions and economic development. But the prominent neoconservatives who supported the war stood largely outside this debate, and one is hard-pressed to find much discussion of the concrete mechanics of how the United States would promote either democratic institutions or economic development. The Kristol-Kagan volume *Present Dangers*, for example, has a discussion of tools to be used to promote democracy around the world; these consist of, first and foremost, the ability to project military power, followed by allies and ballistic missile defense.[4] There is not even a nod toward policy instruments that are critical in helping to bring about political transitions, such as the State Department, the U.S. Agency for International Development, or multilateral institutions like the IMF or World Bank. *The Weekly Standard* focused its advocacy during the Clinton administration on increasing American defense spending, not on promoting new approaches to post-conflict reconstruction, economic development, civil society support, public diplomacy, and the like. These neoconservatives seemed to have assumed that the institutions would somehow take care of themselves once the United States had done the heavy lifting of coercive regime change.

The history of thinking on development since post–World War II decolonization is littered with failed attempts to properly conceptualize the development process and marked by an absence of tools with which outside donors could actually affect development outcomes. It is useful at the outset to separate economic and political development, since the intellectual histories of these two complementary aspects of modernization have taken somewhat different paths, though the two strands had converged somewhat by the 1990s, with interesting implications for future policy.

Economic Development

Thinking on economic development has gone through a series of distinct stages since the dissolution of European colonial empires that began in the late 1940s. Under the early influence of the Harrod-Domar growth model, there was a widespread belief among economists that the chief obstacle to growth in newly independent countries was the so-called investment gap.[5] They tacitly assumed that underdeveloped countries were like developed countries, only lacking in capital. The development strategies promoted by the United States or multilateral agencies like the World Bank consequently focused on large infrastructure projects like dams, roads, and electricity, funneled through existing governments. In the United States there was tremendous optimism that its approach to the electrification of the American South through the Tennessee Valley Authority would provide a model for promoting economic development that could be exported to the newly independent countries. Economic planning was then at its apogee; not just official donors but private organizations like the Ford Foundation gave support to public administration reform and the creation of economic planning agencies.[6]

By the 1970s, there was considerable disillusionment with this approach. Large infrastructural projects did not produce the hoped-for externalities leading to sustained growth, and they were undermined by political instability. In addition, dams and other large engineering projects had unanticipated environmental consequences and fell out of favor during the rise of environmentalism in the 1960s. Much of the support for state institutions ended up reinforcing authoritarian regimes that committed human rights abuses or siphoned off international aid through corruption. Pakistan was a case in point: it received large amounts of aid in the 1950s, then turned to military dictatorship and war with neighboring India in the 1960s.

What the Harrod-Domar model failed to take into account was the fact that underdeveloped countries differed from developed nations in many other ways besides their capital/labor ratios. There were grave deficits not just in physical capital but in human capital as well, which led in the 1960s and 1970s to a new emphasis in development policy on promoting human capital, that is, education. "Sustainable development"—development that minimized environmental consequences of economic growth—became a separate objective of development policy, as did such other goals as population control, rural development, and, with the rise of feminism in the West, women's empowerment. William Easterly's study *The Elusive Quest for Growth* (2001) provides a sobering retrospective of each of these fads in development policy, analyzing why none of them was ever able to create a process of sustained growth.[7]

International donors did have a number of unambiguous successes in promoting development, but it is notable that almost all of them came in the areas of public health and, to some degree, agriculture. Smallpox, polio, tuberculosis, river blindness, and measles have all been either eliminated or greatly reduced as public health problems throughout the developing world, while the green revolution in India and elsewhere was started with help from outside foundations and funders.[8] The latter's ability to promote across-the-board, sustained economic growth, on the other hand, has been much more limited. The rapidly developing countries in East Asia did well on their own; elsewhere, there was little correlation between levels of international investment and positive outcomes.

American policy approaches to development were heavily driven by the needs of American foreign policy, since the United States at that time saw itself locked in a deadly competition with the communist world for influence over developing countries.

Academic theorizing and practical policy making came together in the work of people like Walt Rostow, whose 1960 book *The Stages of Economic Growth* became a template for promoting development during the Kennedy and Johnson administrations.[9] U.S.-Soviet competition culminated in the rival nation-building strategies pursued by North and South Vietnam. With the South Vietnamese defeat in the Vietnam War, Americans' self-confidence that they had a viable theory of political modernization collapsed.

The penultimate fad to hit development policy before the Iraq war was the return to economic orthodoxy in the 1980s. The Reagan and Thatcher revolutions in the political world were accompanied and underpinned by changing intellectual currents that shifted the desired balance between state and market strongly in favor of the latter. Economic planning fell out of favor both in the developed and the less developed world and was replaced by a strong emphasis on free markets and global economic integration. The seemingly miraculous rise of export-oriented East Asian fast developers like South Korea, Taiwan, and Hong Kong reinforced this intellectual trend.

The problem with the return to economic orthodoxy was not that the underlying concepts were wrong; in Chile market liberalization worked quite well. The problem was rather that without strong institutions and political will the policies could not be adopted or implemented properly. In sub-Saharan Africa, governments were largely successful in fending off pressures for policy reform under the endless series of structural adjustment loans offered them by international lending agencies in the 1980s and 1990s.[10]

Indeed, it is in Africa that the overall conceptual and policy failure of Western development strategies is most painfully evident. Despite large levels of outside donor assistance and advice for three decades, per capita incomes in most of the region shrank. African states that had always been weak deteriorated and, in the cases of Somalia, Liberia, and Sierra Leone, disappeared entirely. Indeed, well-intended Western development policies may have made things worse in many cases by creating the donor-funded equivalent of the "natural resource curse" that permitted African governments to evade the need for internal reform, or by strengthening bad governments.[11]

The mid- to late 1990s saw yet another shift in thinking about development policy, one that this time emphasized the importance of institutions. Institutions (that is, formal and informal rules constraining individual choice) had been relatively neglected in neoclassical economics until the rise of the so-called new institutional economics associated with the economic historian Douglass North. Institutional economics arose fortuitously out of theorizing about the firm and became the dominant mode by which economists conceptualized the phenomena of hierarchy that political scientists had traditionally analyzed using different terminology. There is now a substantial empirical literature demonstrating the importance of institutions like property rights, credible enforcement, and rule of law as conditions of successful development. The findings of Easterly and Levine are particularly relevant insofar as they show that natural resource endowments are important to development outcomes primarily as they affect institutional development.[12]

The shift in focus to institutions and, more broadly, the political dimensions of development is long overdue. I have argued elsewhere that the difference in development outcomes between East Asia and Latin America since the 1970s is largely due to the greater competence and strength of state institutions in the former region, rather than to market-friendly policies. There are too many examples of countries with otherwise good prospects whose development was undermined by rapacious leaders, ethnic conflict, internal or external war, or other purely political factors. Good policies, including efforts to reduce the size of the state sector through privatization and deregulation, themselves presuppose strong residual enforcement capability on the part of states.[13]

It is important, however, to put institutions in proper perspective and not make institutional development the latest silver bullet that will solve the problem of economic growth. Institutions are one of many dimensions of development; resources in the form of investment capital, good economic policies, geography, disease burdens, and the like all contribute to development outcomes.

The other critical limitation of the new emphasis on institutions is that while we understand their importance in promoting economic development and can figure out how they work where they exist, we know relatively little about how to create or strengthen them in societies where they are nonexistent or weak. This is not to say that we have *no* knowledge: there are certain areas such as central banking or financial systems more generally where universal templates exist and outside technocrats can bring about substantial improvements in state capacity. But there are other public sector activities, such as establishing a rule of law or promoting primary and secondary education, where universally applicable designs do not exist; these are consequently less susceptible to outside technocratic solutions.

Furthermore, establishing or reforming institutions is almost always more of a political than a technocratic problem. For example, poor fiscal management (such as governments spending more than they take in through tax revenues or else spending public money for private purposes) continually bedevils many developing countries. The reason this happens, however, is only partly a matter of not having the organization and technology to track budgets. More often the problem comes from politicians who want to use public money to maintain patronage networks that are critical to their political survival. Asking them to be fiscally responsible may be tantamount to asking them to commit political suicide, something they are understandably reluctant to do. Fixing this problem therefore requires a political solution, like developing a local constituency in favor of fiscal reform, or otherwise eliminating the political support for the recalcitrant political groups. Sometimes these groups are so entrenched that the problem is essentially unsolvable, at least through external pressure. In the absence of internal political demand for reform, it may never be possible to get the institutions right.

Political Development

Political development is understood to be the creation of formal state institutions of increasing complexity and scope that serve either to promote collective action or to mitigate social conflict. Political development is a superset of democracy promotion: while the development of democratic institutions like legislatures and elections constitutes political development, authoritarian governments can be more or less developed. Before you can have a democracy, you have to have a state: state-building is an activity that overlaps only partially with democracy promotion.[14]

The trajectory of thinking about political development parallels and is closely related to that of economic development, since the two are intertwined in a common process of modernization. American theories of modernization had their origins in the classics of late-nineteenth-century European sociology like the works of Henry Maine, Ferdinand Tönnies, Emile Durkheim, and Max Weber, all of whom supplied concepts—status/contract; *Gemeinschaft/Gesellschaft*; mechanical/organic solidarity; charismatic/bureaucratic-rational authority—by which to understand the modernization process. These ideas migrated from Europe to the United States, sometimes literally in the heads of refugees from Hitler's Europe, and came to settle in places like the Harvard Department of Comparative Politics, the MIT Center for International Studies, or the Social Science Research Council's Committee on Comparative Politics.[15] Talcott Parsons, Edward Shils, Daniel Lerner, Lucian Pye, Gabriel Almond, David Apter, and Walt Rostow all saw themselves as part of a common effort to develop an integrated theory of development that would not only explain the transition from traditional to modern societies but also provide practical advice to American foreign policy makers on how to bring this about.

Like economic development, theories of political development began to crumble in the 1960s in the face of coups, insurgencies, corruption, and authoritarian setbacks. On the left, critics asserted that modernization theory enshrined the single pattern of American development as one that should normatively guide the developing world, something that was regarded by its opponents as ethnocentric and myopic about the realities of non-Western societies. On the right, Samuel Huntington argued in his 1968 landmark work, *Political Order in Changing Societies*, that political decay was as likely as political development. Excessively fast socioeconomic modernization could outrun political development and produce disorder and violence.[16] Modernization no longer appeared to be an integrated process of economic, social, and political change but rather a set of disparate activities that could spin out of control. The policy implication of Huntington's work was that the development of strong political authority was necessary for economic development and needed to precede democracy.

In the wake of the Third Wave of democratization and the collapse of the Soviet Union, theorists have begun reviving a model of political development that runs throughout the "democratic transition" literature. In this model democratic transition is seen as having opening, breakthrough, and consolidation phases. The opening comes as a result of cleavages between hard-liners and soft-liners in the authoritarian government; the soft-liners form pacts with members of the opposition that then make possible the breakthrough to a new democratic regime. The consolidation phase requires neutralizing the remaining hard-liners, and then building institutions to support the new democratic order. This literature was based initially on the experience of southern Europe and Latin America, but it is applicable to certain Eastern European transitions as well.[17]

This democratic transitions literature amounts to something less than a comprehensive theory of political development. It is very specific to certain regions of the world. It fails to answer the question of why soft-liners appear in certain societies and not others, why some societies are willing to work out "pacted" transitions, rather than settling things violently, and why some societies are able to evolve multiparty democracy while others remain dominated by old elites.

As Thomas Carothers points out, there is at times a hidden

developmental assumption that creates inevitable pressures to shift from authoritarian to democratic government; when political progress toward democracy has stalled, or even reversed, countries are still said to be "in transition."[18] Carothers argues that many of these so-called transitional societies may not be moving toward democracy at all but are rather content to remain in a gray zone between authoritarian and democratic government.

To be fair, the assumption of inevitable democratic transition is more often made by politicians and practitioners, who want to be able to speak hopefully about their efforts to promote democracy and political reform around the world, than by academic analysts. Although there is an inner logic to the economic development process—captured by the various growth models used by economists—it is much less clear that a similar logic exists for political development.

To the extent that there is a coherent theory of political development, the process is likely to be based on one of three drivers. The first is the empirical linkage that exists between economic development and democracy. Adam Przeworksi and Fernando Limongi have shown that although transitions to democracy occur with equal frequency at any level of development, they are much less likely to be reversed once a country has passed a level of development of approximately \$6,000 per capita GDP. This explains the correlation between development and democracy first noted by Lipset and suggests that political development will flow from successful economic development.[19]

This theory is good as far as it goes, and it is broadly accepted among political scientists, but it does not explain how political development happens in very poor countries well below the $6,000 per capita threshold. Indeed, if recent theories about the importance of institutions for economic development are correct, a serious chicken-and-egg problem emerges: for countries close to or above the $6,000 per capita threshold, economic development drives political development, but for countries well below it, political development drives economic development. There is no theory of how and why political development occurs in very poor countries.

A second mechanism driving political development is some form of evolutionary competition and emulation whereby societies observe one another and adopt institutions that promote broadly desirable goals like economic development or social justice.[20] The historian Charles Tilly, in his work on European state formation, suggests one specific version of this. He argues that the need to create large-standing armies among Europe's decentralized political units, as well as the economies of scale in commerce offered by cities, led to a competitive process of state growth and consolidation. There are examples of competition driving political development from other parts of the world: the Japanese saw that the society from which Commodore Perry came had something that theirs did not and embarked on a crash course of modernization to maintain their political independence. On the other hand, as Douglass North himself has pointed out, societies fall into cognitive traps in which they either don't understand that they have fallen behind, or they misdiagnose the source of their lack of development, and thus fail to emulate more successful competitive models for long periods of time. In parts of the world like sub-Saharan Africa, endemic violence and military competition have not lead to state formation as in Europe, but rather to chaos and social breakdown.[21]

A final driver of political development lies in the realm of ideas. There is simply no other legitimating set of ideas besides liberal democracy that is broadly accepted in the world today.[22] Feckless authoritarians must themselves adopt the language of democratic transition to legitimate their rule, even if in reality that power rests on patronage, kinship, ethnicity, or other narrow principles. Thus while individual rulers like Turkmenistan's Saparmurat Niyazov or Belarus's Alexander Lukashenko have no intention of moving their countries toward democracy, they themselves remain vulnerable because their regimes are based on no governing set of ideas that animate loyalty or structure authority.

But though there may not be a strong grand theory of political development at this point, there is a huge pool of accumulated practical experience concerning political development strategies. In addition to the democratic transition literature, there has been among political scientists a revival in the past two decades of institutionalism, in which the state is no longer regarded as a passive object of social pressures but viewed as an autonomous and active shaper of outcomes.[23] This has led to a substantial literature on institutional design, concerning such issues as the relative merits of presidential versus parliamentary systems, how executive power interacts with electoral systems, advantages and disadvantages of different forms of federalism, and so forth. There is in addition a growing literature on democracy promotion itself; that is, on what strategies and policies seem to work best in promoting democratic development in authoritarian or transitional societies.[24]

The American Experience in Promoting Democracy and Political Development

The best way to study the prospects and limitations of strategies for promoting democracy is to look back at historical efforts the United States has undertaken, either nation-building exercises or more arms-length attempts to promote the democratic transitions. What one finds is that the record in nation-building is mixed: there are a few successes and a large number of failures; and where the successes occurred, they required an extraordinary level of effort and attention.

On the other hand, the United States often played a decisive arms-length role in promoting Third Wave transitions to democracy. The United States and the international community together have developed an impressive range of political tools for supporting democratic regime change since the early 1980s. In virtually every case, the basic impetus for regime change came from within the target society and not from external pressure. The United States can be extremely helpful to an organic process of democratic transition, but it has little leverage in the absence of relatively strong domestic actors.

Before the Iraq war, President Bush and other members of his administration noted that the United States had successfully democratized other aggressive dictatorships, particularly Germany and Japan, where America "did not leave behind occupying armies" but "constitutions and parliaments." This was true, but the examples were rather misleading. Germany and Japan *were* transformed into model democracies after 1945, but they started out as highly developed countries with strong states whose cores for the most part survived the war intact. They were, moreover, thoroughly defeated societies that had turned decisively against the political forces that led them to war.[25]

Better comparators would have been America's experience in governing the Philippines, the many Caribbean and Latin American interventions under the Monroe Doctrine, or the intervention in Bosnia, where the U.S. record has been decidedly mixed. The United States ruled the Philippines for almost fifty years, yet the record of democracy after independence up to 1986 was shaky, and it remains one of the least successful ASEAN (Association of Southeast Asian Nations) states in terms of economic development. The United States intervened repeatedly in Cuba, Nicaragua, the Dominican Republic, and Haiti and did not succeed in leaving behind strong institutions in any of these countries. The intervention in Bosnia was successful insofar as it ended the conflict and restored Bosnia to prewar levels of economic activity, but it required substantial resources and a high level of international involvement. More important, the underlying political problem has not been resolved: the prospect that the international community will dismantle the Office of the High Representative that rules the country on its behalf anytime soon is not good.[26]

As America's experience in Iraq has shown quite vividly, democratic regime change via military intervention and occupation is extremely costly and uncertain, and it is not an instrument that is ever likely to be used routinely in the future. On the other hand, the United States and other developed democracies played important and in some cases decisive roles in helping along many of the democratic transitions that occurred from the early 1970s on. These were all the product of soft rather than hard power—that is, they were brought about by instruments like diplomatic pressure, funding to prodemocracy groups, public diplomacy, training, and the like.

The first case of successful transition occurred at the beginning of the Third Wave, when the German party institutes (the Friedrich Ebert Stiftung and the Konrad Adenauer Stiftung) gave material support to their counterpart parties in Portugal after the fall of the dictatorship of António de Oleveira Salazar. Portugal endured a brief period of quasi–civil war in 1974–75, and the Portuguese Communist Party might well have seized power after a coup by left-wing military officers but for the external support received by Portugal's democratic parties.

The success of the German *Stiftungen* in abetting the Portuguese transition was one of the factors that inspired the creation of the National Endowment for Democracy (NED) in the United States in the early 1980s. During the Cold War, the United States had supported democratic trade unions, magazines, political parties, and the like in its struggle for influence against the Soviet Union. Some of this support had been funneled through the CIA, which in certain instances gave support to decidedly nondemocratic groups. As a result of the revelations concerning CIA covert operations in the 1970s and the activities of the Church Committee that exposed many of them, the United States put sharp limits on this type of activity and decided to bring democracy support out into the open. In addition to the NED, the U.S. Agency for International Development (USAID) developed a Democracy and Governance branch, while the State Department set up a bureau for Democracy, Human Rights, and Labor that is now overseen by the undersecretary for global affairs.

American influence played a critical role in several subsequent democratic transitions. A major shift took place in U.S. policy during the mid- to late 1980s. Previously, anticommunism and foreign policy realism had led Washington to support or at least acquiesce in the rule of a number of authoritarian states on the grounds that these governments were the lesser of two evils.[27] But with the tempering of the Cold War, the perceived risk of supporting democratic forces on the left diminished and the United States increasingly used its influence to nudge dictators out of power. With support from the United Nations, the United States brokered a negotiated end to the civil war in El Salvador and, after supporting the Contras in Nicaragua, brought about a democratic transition there as well.[28] In the Philippines the United States played a critical role in easing Ferdinand Marcos out of office during the "people power" revolution following the assassination of Benigno Aquino in 1986. The following year, it used its influence to prevent the South Korean military from cracking down on student and trade union protesters, and facilitated that country's move to free legislative elections. And in 1988 Washington quietly dropped its support for Chile's Augusto Pinochet when he unexpectedly called for a referendum on his rule, and pressed him to accept the results of the "no" vote.

American hard power played an important role in these transitions: military relationships with South Korea, Taiwan, and the Philippines gave Washington great leverage. Coercive regime change was successfully employed in Panama in 1991. But the United States developed an array of other tools during this period. Perhaps the most important was the capability of monitoring elections through the use of election observers, exit polls, and media coverage. Early efforts to monitor elections in Central America during the 1980s were marked by limited capabilities, but by the end of the 1990s the United States, the United Nations, and a number of nongovernmental organizations (NGOs) like the Carter Center, Democracy Watch, IFES, Freedom House, and the Eurasia Foundation had developed sophisticated techniques for monitoring the fairness of elections taking place under semi-authoritarian circumstances.[29] Democracy-support organizations like the NED and NGOs like the American Center for Labor Solidarity (affiliated with the AFL-CIO) were critical in providing support to the Solidarity labor union in Poland; over the years these organizations grew into a much broader instrument for civil society development. Broadcasting, through agencies like Radio Free Europe/Radio Liberty and the Voice of America, was an important means of providing people in the communist world with alternative sources of information about their own countries and the outside world.

By the early twenty-first century, a vast international infrastructure had emerged to help societies make the initial transition from authoritarian government to democracy, and to help consolidate democratic institutions once the initial transition was completed. The impact of these international soft-power instruments was clearly evident in the three major democratic transitions that took place in Europe in the new millennium— the fall of Slobodan Miloševiç in Serbia in 2000, the Rose Revolution in Georgia in 2003, and the Orange Revolution in Ukraine in 2004–5. The pattern in each of these cases was the same: a corrupt and/or semi-authoritarian leader held an election that was rigged or falsified; demonstrations broke out to protest the election results; the population mobilized against the former leader, resulting finally in nonviolent, democratic regime change.

External support was critical in each of these cases. Without a sophisticated network of international election monitors who could be mobilized quickly, it would have been impossible to demonstrate the falsification of election results. Without independent media, it would have been impossible to produce mass mobilizations, and these organizations (such as *Maidan*, *Ostriv*, and *Ukrainska Pravda*) also received substantial external support. Without the long-term building of civil society organizations that could mobilize to protest the election, street demonstrations and direct action would not have materialized. In Serbia student groups like Otpor received support from a variety of Western democracy-promotion organizations, including NED, the International Republican Institute, and USAID. Ukrainian civil society organizations involved in the Orange Revolution, including the Ukrainian Youth Association, Young Rukh, and the School for Policy Analysis of the Kyiv-Mohyla Academy, had been NED grantees for many years. The philanthropist George Soros's Open Society Institute also played a significant role in providing assistance in all these countries.

Recent cases of successful democracy promotion have had three characteristics. First, the initiative has to come from within the society in question. Unless there are strong, unified indigenous groups willing to resist the former regime, regime change will not occur. Outside funders and organizers are critical in helping to strengthen these organizations, but the latter must sink their own roots in their own societies. Outside funders cannot by themselves determine the timing of democratic transitions, which are sparked by specific events like an assassination or a fraudulent election that becomes a source of outrage and mobilization.

In addition, external support works only in semi-authoritarian regimes that feel the need to stage elections and permit some degree of freedom for civil society groups to organize. The Serbian, Georgian, and Ukrainian transitions came about in the wake of contested elections and would not have occurred in their absence. Totalitarian regimes like Saddam Hussein's Iraq or most former communist countries before 1989 would not be vulnerable to this kind of action.

Finally, the receptivity of indigenous prodemocracy forces to outside support, and particularly support from the United States, is very much dependent on the society's specific history and the kind of nationalism at work. Most of the Eastern European countries transitioning to democracy after 1989, as well as Serbia, Georgia, and Ukraine, had populations that wanted for the most part to join Western Europe and the broader community of developed democracies. They did not regard themselves as failed or humiliated imperial powers and were happy to receive support from the United States; to the extent they were threatened by anything, it was by Russian nationalism. The same would not necessarily be the case in countries like Russia or China, which have their own memories of dominance and hegemony, or in certain parts of the Arab world that are conflicted about the kind of society they seek to become and their relationship to a U.S.-led West.[30]

Rethinking Development

Development, both economic and political, has always been some-thing of a stepchild in American foreign policy. Foreign policy has revolved around activities like fighting wars, balancing threats, or negotiating agreements. Development has always come as an afterthought, a kind of mop-up activity pursued when the "seri-ous" players left the stage. During the Cold War and the heyday of classical modernization theory, development was taken a bit more seriously: it was seen as a means of inoculating populations from the appeal of communism, a way to stabilize allies and anchor American influence around the world. But with the de-cline in Washington's self-confidence in the ability of the United States to promote successful development, it came to be seen as less and less central to American purposes. Foreign aid was at-tacked on the right as a giveaway to corrupt foreign leaders and on the left as an instrument of American imperialism. The U.S. Agency for International Development was subordinated to the State Department, had its budget sharply reduced, and saw steady attrition of much of its personnel. When the Clinton adminis-tration intervened in Haiti and the Balkans for largely humani-tarian reasons, it was attacked for trivializing foreign policy as "social work."[31]

After September 11 and the Iraq war, development recovered some of its lost status. It was initially seen as a way of fighting terrorism, a means of "draining the swamp" that fed Muslim rage and alienation. The Bush administration proposed doubling the amount of money going to foreign aid in its first post–September 11 budget, as well as increasing the U.S. contribution to the fight against HIV/AIDS in Africa. With the difficulties experienced in pacifying Iraq, the Bush administration recognized that reconstruction was not a lesser included case of active combat but an activity that had, alas, its own requirements and logic. By the time of Bush's second inaugural, the political side of development—democracy promotion—had been elevated, rhetorically at least, to the central position in U.S. foreign policy.

If the United States wants to make development a key component of its foreign policy and not simply an afterthought, it is important not to load onto it expectations that will inevitably be disappointed. This means defining objectives clearly and examining in a hard-headed way what instruments the United States has available for achieving them.

On the political side of development, the United States ought to set as its objective the promotion of good governance, not just democracy. As noted above, political development is a superset of democracy promotion. It involves things like state-building and the creation of effective institutions that are conditions of democratic government but not necessarily democratic in themselves. Fareed Zakaria is right that, where possible, a liberal rule of law is initially more critical to economic growth than democratic political participation, and that modernizing authoritarians might be preferable in some cases to feckless democracies.[32]

Deferring democracy in favor of liberal authoritarianism is

not, however, particularly useful as a general strategy. Liberal authoritarians are, in the first place, hard to find; they seem for some reason to be concentrated primarily in East Asia. Most developing country dictators are both incompetent at promoting growth and corrupt to boot. Reformers who want to promote liberal rule of law, by contrast, tend also to want democracy. But there is a deeper connection at work. Good governance is ultimately not possible without democracy and public participation: the quality of a bureaucracy that is insulated from public scrutiny and oversight deteriorates over time; corruption can be reined in only if a broader public is made aware of its existence and demands better performance from public officials. Without democratic legitimacy, authoritarian rulers will not survive inevitable setbacks and crises.

The United States should promote the economic development of poor countries both as an end in itself and as a complement to U.S. efforts to promote democracy, since democracy is much easier to consolidate against the backdrop of economic growth. There is both a moral and a practical reason for doing this. The moral argument is straightforward: it is simply unacceptable for the richest and most powerful country in human history to be indifferent to the plight of countries that not only lack its human and social resources but are moving steadily backward in their standards of living. If we want to live in a world where many others share our values and institutions, our prosperity needs to be more broadly distributed as well.

The practical motive has to do not with terrorism but with the background conditions that facilitate terrorism and other threats to global order. The September 2002 *National Security Strategy of the United States* puts the issue quite well: "Poverty does not make poor people into terrorists and murderers. Yet poverty, weak institutions, and corruption can make weak states vulnerable to terrorist networks and drug cartels within their borders." The effort that the United States is seen to put into development affects how the country is perceived around the world. The United States is increasingly seen as isolated, self-absorbed, and interested in other countries' problems only when its own citizens are in some way involved. There are many middle-sized and smaller countries that could get away with this kind of posture. But it is difficult for the United States to do so if it wants to lead by example and be an inspiration to others.

If the United States were to make a new start at promoting economic development, however, how could it approach the problem in ways that might actually help poor countries? The economist Jeffrey Sachs has been relentless in calling on the United States to meet the Millennium Development Goal of committing 0.7 percent of its GDP to development assistance, which would more than triple the current level of outlays. It is true that the United States has become steadily less generous in this area; at .17 it ranks at the bottom of the twenty-two members of the Organisation for Economic Co-operation and Development (OECD) in terms of percent of GDP devoted to overseas development assistance (ODA). Even if one adds in private charity to this amount, the U.S. ranking rises only to twenty-first out of twenty-two.[33]

But before the U.S. Congress can be persuaded to increase spending on development assistance, it needs to be convinced that the money will buy something useful in terms of actual outcomes for poor people in developing countries. There are some things that money can buy and others that it can't. Antiretroviral drugs for people living on a dollar a day, research and development of antimalarial drugs, bed nets, and the like are all expensive goods that private markets will not produce on their own, and for which there is a good case for public subsidy.

On the other hand, these drugs will not reach their intended recipients and will not be administered properly without a strong public health infrastructure in each local country, systematic public education, and an institutionalized effort to follow up on initial donor efforts. Oftentimes, because that infrastructure is lacking, or because local officials are corrupt or lack capacity, aid fails to reach its intended targets. This then leads outside aid agencies to try to deliver services directly by bypassing local governments, a procedure that speeds service delivery but has the long-term effect of undermining the public authorities of the recipient nation, as workers desert the public sector for substantially better paid employment with foreign donors and NGOs. When foreign assistance is channeled through local governments, it is often used for political purposes (such as advantaging one ethnic group or tribe over another) or else ends up distorting and undermining local markets.[34]

Conservative critics of traditional foreign assistance are right about certain things: a great many taxpayer dollars earmarked for poor people in the developing world have ended up in the hands of developed-world contractors or private companies or else have been siphoned off by local officials. If they don't go into the proverbial Swiss bank account, then they serve other uses that are downright destructive, like buying weapons. There is a real risk that if the United States were to spend as much money on foreign assistance as Sachs would like, these funds would outstrip local capacity and actually hurt the long-term development prospects of the people they were designed to help.

There is thus a strong case to be made that the United States ought to be more generous in supporting not just political but economic development around the world. But it needs to be discriminating in the use of its money and should focus its efforts on building stronger institutions and governance in poor countries. Long-term attention to institutions and politics will have two benefits, given the convergence between the economic and political development agendas. The rule of law is extremely important for creating a climate in which investment and economic growth can take place; it also constitutes the "liberal" part of a liberal democracy. Controlling rent-seeking and clientelism, ensuring that public monies are spent on public goods and not on patronage, and reining in rapacious corruption simultaneously promote development and help legitimate democratic political systems.

Since the 1980s, international financial institutions like the IMF and World Bank have sought to use conditionality in structural adjustment loans as a means of artificially stimulating demand for reform in countries where it is low. Conditionality has had some success in promoting policy reform in the area of macroeconomic stabilization, but it has had much less impact on long-term institutional development in areas like rule of law and anticorruption. Policy reform involves short-term decisions in areas like interest rates or subsidies that are clearly within the purview of governments; institutional reform by contrast involves a shifting of the balance of power among political actors that often threatens entrenched interests. External incentives have to be much stronger in the latter case, and in either event they can be effective only if there are local political actors who have their own reasons for bringing them about.

There are a number of reasons why conditionality in structural-adjustment lending seldom generates sufficient demand for institutional reform. First, the conditionality is usually front-loaded, with money disbursed on a promise to carry out the conditions rather than as a reward for actual performance. Lucy's promise not to pull away the football is usually sufficient to keep Charlie Brown returning for another kick. Second, the judgment as to whether conditions have been met is corruptible; since the international financial institutions and donor agencies have their own incentives to push loans on their clients regardless of actual performance, they are often complicit in watering down the criteria for aid. Third, the multiplicity of lenders and donor objectives has meant that even if one lender pulls the plug on a particular country, another will step in and make up the shortfall. And finally, the lenders themselves seek to micromanage reform, establishing long lists of sometimes mutually contradictory conditions that often fail to take account of the political and social realities of the country in question. Recipient countries that try to meet lender conditions often stimulate social unrest and backlash, which then undermines the whole reform process. Those that avoid this pitfall become tied up in donor-imposed red tape.

One of the most successful engines of institutional reform has been the European Union's accession process, which has transformed the institutional landscape in Eastern Europe and beyond. The reason it has been successful is that E.U. accession is a form of conditionality that avoids many of the pitfalls of structural adjustment lending: E.U. membership provides a large political and economic incentive to reform; it is completely backloaded, rewarding countries only after reforms are completed; and the accession criteria are relatively transparent and hard to dilute. The initiative, moreover, always lies with the countries wanting to join the European Union; if they don't have the political will to join, no one is forcing them to. Most E.U. member states would actually prefer that the club be kept smaller and more exclusive.

The Bush administration's Millennium Challenge Account (MCA) was initially designed to overcome the limitations of structural-adjustment lending on the part of multilateral institutions like the World Bank.[35] It specified a series of governance indicators as the basis for reform and sought to back-load conditionality by specifying a series of governance thresholds that countries would have to meet before qualifying for the program. The "foundation" model for aid put the burden properly on the recipient countries to design and execute the proposals for assistance, rather than having the aid agency decide for them what they needed.

While the MCA's approach to development is innovative, the Bush administration's follow-through has been less than stellar. When the program was first announced in March 2002, the administration proposed an annual funding level of $5 billion, which would have effectivcly doubled the level of U.S. ODA to poor countries. In 2005, however, Congress funded only $1.75 billion of the aid. By the beginning of its second term, the administration had not disbursed a single loan, and was ready to prequalify only two countries, Honduras and Madagascar. Critics charged, moreover, that the governance criteria had been set in such a way that the only countries that could qualify for funding were ones that didn't need it because they already had good governance.

The other problematic feature of the MCA was that it was designed as a new agency, wholly American owned and funded. Since one of the great banes of foreign assistance is lack of donor coordination, it appeared that the MCA might simply add yet another set of bureaucratic requirements to the existing plethora of donor decrees. Moreover, the MCA's relationship to the rest of the U.S. government's activities in related areas was unclear: was it meant to complement or ultimately replace the ongoing work of USAID?

A lesson that clearly emerges from the history of successful development in the late twentieth century—from Korea and Taiwan to Botswana and Uganda—is that institutions will not be created unless there is a strong internal demand for them. Bad governance, weak institutions, political corruption, and patronage exist because certain powerful political actors have a strong self-interest in the status quo. Unless political will can be generated from within the society to overcome these actors, outside pressure is seldom sufficient by itself to dislodge them.

There is genuine institutional reform going on in many developing countries that flies under the radar screen of even informed foreign observers. Federal elections in Mexico, for example, used to be brazenly manipulated by the long-time ruling Institutional Revolutionary Party (PRI), which up through the early 1990s had a hammerlock on Mexican politics. In 1996, however, Mexico reformed its Federal Electoral Institute (Instituto Federal Electoral, or IFE), which since then has monitored federal elections, provided voter and citizen education, and fined political parties for violations of campaign finance rules. Today IFE is a large organization, with 13,000 employees and branches in every Mexican state and city, and Mexican federal elections are at least as clean as their American counterparts. All of this was done by the Mexicans themselves, with relatively little help from outside election specialists.

Reforming American Soft-Power Institutions

If the United States is to promote political and economic development, it needs not simply to reconceptualize the development problem around the question of institutions, but also to reform those American departments and agencies that are meant to promote development and project American "soft power." Joseph Nye, a professor and former Clinton administration official, has coined this term to describe the ability to get what you want not through military and economic coercion but rather through the positive attraction of your values and society.[36] This definition is not wholly suitable to encompass the sorts of institutions in question; loan conditionality on the part of development agencies, for example, is often perceived as coercive by aid recipients. It is nonetheless a useful label for agencies like the State Department, the U.S. Agency for International Development, the Millennium Challenge Corporation, and the various broadcasting and democracy-promotion organizations that seek to shape global politics through nonmilitary means.

In contrast to the U.S. military, which used the period after the end of the Vietnam War to remake itself into a highly motivated and well-led institution, the soft-power agencies in the U.S.

government's foreign policy establishment were, before September 11, underfunded, demoralized, and disorganized. Substantial new money has gone into them since then, but the results have been less than satisfying because the agencies face deeper problems having to do with mission and institutional culture.

Take an issue like democracy promotion in the Middle East, which the Bush administration has made the centerpiece of its regional policy. The way that the U.S. government is organized for democracy promotion leaves a great deal to be desired. Authority is split across a wide variety of agencies. These include the Office of Democracy and Governance at the U.S. Agency for International Development (as well as USAID's regional bureaus), which is in dollar terms the largest dispenser of funds; the National Endowment for Democracy and institutes like the National Democratic Institute (NDI) and the International Republican Institute (IRI) that operate under its umbrella; and the Middle East Partnership Initiative (MEPI) and the Office of Democracy, Human Rights, and Labor (DRL) at the Department of State. Public diplomacy is an integral part of democracy promotion, and in this area authority is similarly diffused between the State Department's undersecretary for public diplomacy and public affairs and the Broadcasting Board of Governors, under which operate a slew of individual agencies including Voice of America, Radio SAWA, Radio Free Europe/Radio Liberty, Alhurra, Radio Farda, and the like. There is no overall coordination of their dif-

ferent activities, meaning that many of them are duplicative, un-
coordinated, and frequently at cross purposes.

The problems with American soft power lie deeper than simple
institutional fragmentation. The U.S. Agency for International
Development, for example, has never been able to cultivate the
professionalism and pride of either the State Department or the
military services, and in the 1990s it was subordinated altogether
to the Department of State.[37] Its budget has been earmarked to
death by Congress, which mandates that it support favorite programs of particular members of Congress. USAID underwent
steady losses of personnel during the 1990s and lost much of its
technical capacity to oversee development projects. As a result, it
depends heavily on a host of for-profit contractors like Chemon-
ics International or Bearing Point or on nonprofit NGOs to actually deliver services in developing countries.

The lack of understanding of how to use American soft-power
institutions became glaringly obvious during the reconstruction
of Iraq. The United States has been involved in a large number
of nation-building projects since the Reconstruction of the South
after the Civil War and was engaged with particular intensity in
places like Haiti, Somalia, Bosnia, and Kosovo. Very little institutional learning took place during these exercises, however. The
Clinton administration tried to impose some order on a chaotic
interagency process by promulgating Presidential Decision Directive 56, a document that defined agency roles and missions

during a complex post-conflict reconstruction project. Even this small degree of institutional learning was tossed out by the Bush administration before the Afghan war, with the result that the administration went into two large-scale nation-building projects in Afghanistan and Iraq without the benefit of much of the accumulated knowledge that existed in the U.S. government on the subject. The Bush administration has tacitly acknowledged these weaknesses by establishing a new office in the State Department of the Coordinator for Reconstruction and Stabilization, though whether this is ultimately the best institutional home for this function, and how much authority it will be given, remains to be seen.

The obvious difficulties that the Bush administration faced in Iraq have led to a series of studies on how to reorganize the U.S. government to do better next time. A group from the Center for Global Development, for example, has urged the creation of a cabinet-level Department of Development, comparable to Britain's Department for International Development, to oversee American development activities.[38] It is doubtful, however, that the U.S. Congress will consider in effect raising USAID to cabinet status unless it has a stronger sense that such a move will produce results. In fact, a different and more radical type of surgery might be appropriate. Rather than enlarging USAID, it might make more sense to break out the really effective parts of the agency, such as the Disaster and Reconstruction Teams or the Office of Transition Initiatives, and roll them into a single agency for reconstruction, leaving long-term development to a revamped Millennium Challenge Corporation.[39]

If the United States is to foster economic and political development through a focus on institution-building, it needs to take a dramatically different approach. The MCA model is fundamentally sound, but Washington would have to agree to fund it adequately in order to give countries a real incentive for joining up. Americans would also have to learn to be patient. They cannot expect measurable year-to-year results, since institution-building often depends on political opportunities and takes time under the best of circumstances. Executed properly, the main work of reform should be undertaken *before* countries qualify for the MCA, using qualification as a back-loaded incentive rather than as a prelude to a donor-micromanaged project.

In rethinking the design of U.S. soft-power institutions, a final issue concerns the way that American agencies would relate to the rest of the world. When designing the Millennium Challenge Account, the Bush administration opted for a new, U.S.-only agency rather than trying to design a more ambitious multilateral institution. The latter could have taken the MCA's novel approach but brought more countries into the funding base, thereby addressing the problem of donor coordination. The administration decided against this option in part because it wanted to keep control (and political credit) in American hands, but also because it was contemptuous of multilateral institutions like the World Bank and thought the United States could do better on its own.

It is not at all clear that this was a good tradeoff. Well into the administration's second term, the MCA is floundering and is likely to be a much more modest initiative than it seemed when first announced in 2002. Instead of trying to reinvent USAID, it might have been better for the United States to try to reinvent the World Bank and other multilateral financial institutions. But the Bush administration has had an aversion to thinking about new multilateral institutions, with the result that it is likely to leave behind no lasting architecture for addressing problems of world order.

6 *Rethinking Institutions for World Order*

The Iraq war exposed the limits of benevolent hegemony on the part of the United States. But it also exposed the limits of existing international institutions, particularly the United Nations, that were favored by the Europeans as the proper framework for legitimate international action. The United Nations was not able either to ratify the U.S. decision to go to war or to stop Washington from acting on its own. From either perspective, it failed.

The world today does not have enough international institutions that can confer legitimacy on collective action, and creating new institutions that will better balance the requirements of legitimacy and effectiveness will be the prime task for the coming generation. As a result of more than two hundred years of political evolution, we have a relatively good understanding of how to create institutions that are rule-bound, accountable, and yet reasonably effective in the vertical silos we call states. What we do not have are adequate institutions of horizontal accountability among states.

The need for horizontal accountability has become particularly critical for two reasons. First, globalization has meant that societies are increasingly interpenetrated economically and culturally; a technological change or new investment thousands of miles away can lead to job losses, new cultural influences, or environmental damage at home. The ability of countries, or, more properly, actors within countries, to affect people outside the sovereign jurisdiction from which they operate has thus increased enormously.

Second, the de facto weight of the United States on the global stage has created an inherent imbalance: the United States can affect many countries around the world without their being able to exercise a reciprocal degree of influence on the United States. This is most glaringly obvious in the military realm, where the United States can change a regime 8,000 miles away. But the disparity exists in a host of other domains, as when an agricultural subsidy or change in trade rules can wipe out an entire sector in a developing country's economy. Few trust the United States to be sufficiently benevolent or wise to use its one-sided influence for everyone's benefit without the subjection of American power to more formal constraints.

The existence of the United Nations is in a way a huge distraction that prevents people on both the right and left from thinking clearly about global governance and international institutions. The Right associates global governance with the United Nations, and because that institution often makes itself an easy target, the Right can reject global governance as a whole. But there is a great deal of global governance in the world today that exists outside the orbit of the United Nations and its allied agencies; everything from bank settlements to communications protocols to safety standards to Internet domain names is set by new and often complex institutions that escape traditional definitions of international cooperation. The old realist model of international relations that sees the world exclusively organized around sovereign nation-states simply does not correspond to the world that is emerging, and it will not be sufficient to meet the needs of legitimacy and effectiveness in international action in the future.

The American Left and many Europeans, on the other hand, overemphasize the importance of the United Nations and place too many hopes in its ability to solve the world's security and economic problems. The fact is that the United Nations, while useful for certain functions like peacekeeping and nation-building, is structurally limited with regard to both legitimacy and effectiveness, and it is doubtful that any set of reforms currently contemplated or politically feasible will solve the organization's problems.

A realistic solution to the problem of international action that is both effective and legitimate will lie in the creation of new institutions and the adaptation of existing ones to new circumstances. An appropriate agenda for American foreign policy will be to promote a world populated by a large number of overlapping and sometimes competitive international institutions, what can be labeled multi-multilateralism. In this world the United Nations would not disappear, but it would become one of several organizations that fostered legitimate and effective international action.

A major problem faced by the United Nations is the question of legitimacy. This problem arises from the fact that its membership is based on formal sovereignty rather than a substantive definition of justice—in particular, it makes no practical demands on its members to be democratic or to respect the human rights of its citizens.[1] This accommodation to the reality of world politics as it existed at the time of the organization's founding has in many ways tainted the subsequent activities of that body, which from the beginning has been populated by authoritarian, abusive, or unrepresentative states.

The ideological conflicts of the Cold War were in the end divisions over basic principles of justice, so it is no surprise that the United Nations was frequently deadlocked and impotent in dealing with security problems. The end of the Cold War aroused hopes that the organization would gain new effectiveness because there would henceforth be greater consensus around broad principles of human rights and democracy. But while most U.N. members paid lip service to these principles, many of them did not remotely live up to them; yet they continued to be treated as members in good standing. Thus could the United States be displaced by Syria on the U.N. Human Rights Commission in 2001 and Libya become its chair in 2003.

Americans are much more likely to point to the organization's lack of democratic legitimacy than are Europeans, a tendency that explains the substantially higher degree of distrust among Americans for the institution and their reluctance to abide by its many pronouncements. Part of this distrust has to do with significant differences between Americans and Europeans over the meaning of democratic sovereignty.

The United States has an abiding belief in constitutional democracy as the source of all legitimacy, and an equal faith in the legitimacy of its own democratic institutions. Many Europeans, by contrast, distrust sovereignty per se because they believe it is a source of conflict and war, based on their experiences during two world wars in the first half of the twentieth century. Many European countries have sought to encase their sovereignties in a series of overlapping institutions, including both the United Nations and the European Union. It is not surprising, then, that Europeans on the whole regard the United Nations as more legitimate than do Americans.

A further source of American distrust of the United Nations arises as a by-product of America's special relationship with Israel and its experience of how the United Nations has dealt with the Arab-Israeli dispute over the years. The General Assembly has passed a number of resolutions regarded by both Israel and the United States as unbalanced or lopsidedly pro-Arab, the most infamous of which was the 1975 "Zionism is racism" resolution.[2] Europeans by contrast tend to place greater blame on Israel for stimulating hostility to itself. Over the years the United States has found itself frequently vetoing Security Council resolutions regarded as biased against Israel, thus habituating itself to standing against majority opinion in that organization.

The second problem with the United Nations has to do with its efficacy as an institution meant to deal with serious security threats. Article 51 authorizations for the use of force must go through the Security Council. But the Security Council, whose membership reflects the winning coalition in World War II, was deliberately designed to be a weak institution: the veto power enjoyed by the five permanent members guaranteed that the Security Council would never act contrary to their national interests. The wartime coalition fell apart in the Cold War, and the Security Council was thereafter never able to agree on responses to serious security threats requiring the use of force. (The sole exception was Korea in 1950, when the Soviet Union made the mistake of walking out of the Security Council, thus allowing the other four members to vote for intervention.) With the Cold War's end, the Security Council united in authorizing U.N. action against Iraq after the country's 1990 invasion of Kuwait. But the organization failed to follow through in enforcing its own disarmament resolutions on Baghdad in the subsequent decade, laying the ground for the American intervention in 2003.

That there are deficiencies in the ability of the United Nations to authorize force to deal with major security issues does not mean that the organization cannot play an important role in post-conflict reconstruction and other nation-building activities. This has indeed happened in the Congo, El Salvador, Mozambique, Eastern Slavonia, Bosnia, and other places. But while the United Nations provides legitimacy and a useful umbrella for organizing international peacekeeping and stabilization operations, even here its limitations are evident. The Security Council's cumbersome decision-making apparatus makes it hard for that body to allocate responsibility for blame in a given conflict and thus to move from peacekeeping to peace enforcement.[3] The United Nations is not a hierarchical organization that is capable of taking decisive action. It necessarily moves by consensus, and it is particularly dependent on its major donors—which in practice means the United States, the Europeans, and Japan—for money, troops, and technical assistance.

Over the years there have been a number of proposals to alter the membership of the Security Council to reflect changes in the distribution of power around the world and thereby improve the Council's perceived legitimacy. It is doubtful whether any of these reform schemes will work, short of a major crisis. Existing members will veto any proposal that will deprive them of their current influence, while new members will inevitably be opposed by other countries that believe themselves equally deserving of a seat.

Even if the membership of the Security Council could be expanded or changed, the problem of collective action will remain.

A larger Security Council with more veto-bearing members will suffer from even greater paralysis than at present. But to change the voting rules from consensus to some form of majority rule risks making the Security Council more active than any of its members would like. The United States in particular, which has found itself isolated in many Security Council votes, is not realistically ever going to approve a change from the unanimity rule. There is a real question, indeed, whether the world would benefit from a supercharged United Nations that could authorize a major use of force under conditions where its constituent members were sharply divided on the wisdom or legitimacy of an action. Most likely it would authorize such a use of force only once before vaporizing.

If the United Nations is not ultimately reformable, what can take its place? The answer is likely to be not a different global institution but rather a multiplicity of international organizations that could provide both power and legitimacy for different types of challenges to world order. Placing all our eggs in the basket of a single, global institution is a formula either for tyranny—were that institution to become truly powerful—or ineffectiveness, which is the current reality of a great deal of U.N. activity. The world is far too diverse and complex to be overseen properly by a single global body. A true liberal principle would argue not for a single, overarching, enforceable liberal order but rather for a diversity of institutions and institutional forms to provide governance across a range of security, economic, environmental, and other issues.

A world of multiple competing and partially overlapping international institutions has already started to take shape over the past decades, primarily in the economic sphere, but with increasing implications for how international political problems will be addressed. All international institutions face the same design tradeoffs that the United States faced in approaching the Iraq war: institutions that are regarded as legitimate (such as the United Nations) are not terribly effective, while those that are effective (the U.S.-led coalition of the willing) are not regarded as legitimate. The demand for effective institutions exists across the board and has produced its own supply in the form of a multiplicity of new forms of international cooperation.

The figure below illustrates this design continuum. At one end are formal, traditional, treaty-based international organizations like the United Nations, the World Bank, and the NATO alliance that correspond to what most people think of when they hear the word *multilateralism*. These institutions are created by sovereign states that delegate powers to international organizations in formal legal agreements. They are transparent insofar as their rules have been explicitly negotiated and agreed to, and they are accountable insofar as they can be disciplined by the states that originally created them.

At the other end of the spectrum are informal types of cooper-

Legitimacy versus Effectiveness
Examples and Types of International Cooperation

United Nations
Intl Telecom Union (ITU)
World Bank
Intergovernmentalism
Intl Org for Standards (ISO)
Soft Law
Bank for Intl Settlements
ICANN
Coalitions of the Willing
Corporate Codes

⟷

Formal	Informal
Transparent	Flexible, fast
Accountable	Non-accountable
Legitimate	Weak legitimacy
Based on sovereign states	Multiple non-state actors

ation that are often not legally grounded in international law, that at times involve parties that are not states as direct participants, and whose rules are often flexible, quickly negotiated, and sometimes unwritten. An example might be a corporate code of conduct negotiated between a clothing manufacturer and a group of unions or nongovernmental organizations purporting to represent the interests of the manufacturer's workers in a developing country. Another example would be what has come to be called soft law, that is, nonbinding agreements like the never-ratified START (Strategic Arms Reduction Talks) Treaty that parties follow for pragmatic rather than legal reasons.[4]

Unlike formal legal institutions, these forms of cooperation are often nontransparent, and are negotiated between parties that lack accountability.[5] On the other hand, international actors resort to this type of cooperation because it is fast, flexible, and relatively easy to negotiate. The clothing manufacturer and its NGO critics, for example, could have gone to the World Trade Organization to have formal rules regarding labor practices attached to trade initiatives, but such an agreement would be difficult if not impossible to negotiate and inflexible once it was in place.

In between these two extremes lie a host of other institutional possibilities. For example, many international standards for products ranging from cameras to plywood are set by the International Organization for Standards (ISO), a body created in 1946 that now coordinates the efforts of more than a hundred national standards–setting bodies. ISO's technical committees, subcommittees, and working groups include not just official standards organizations but representatives of private industry, consumer and business groups, and other parties that might be affected by a given standard.[6]

In themselves, ISO standards constitute private rather than public law: compliance with them is voluntary and the organization has no mechanism of enforcement. On the other hand, ISO standards frequently become public law when they are adopted by states or by supranational organizations like the European Union as the basis for legal commerce, at which point they acquire the weight of state enforcement power.

In addition, there is an entirely separate intermediate realm that Anne-Marie Slaughter labels intergovernmentalism.[7] This comprises understandings and negotiations undertaken by officials representing sovereign states, but ones that are often informally undertaken at intermediate levels of the bureaucracy and that have not been formally vetted through the highest levels of a country's government. The work of intergovernmental networks more typically results in an MOU (memorandum of understanding) than in a formal treaty or agreement, and it is clearly halfway between the two poles of the continuum. That is, an MOU is more legitimate because it is negotiated by sovereign states, but it is less transparent (a U.S. citizen in some cases must file a Freedom of Information request to see the text of an MOU) and less accountable than a formal agreement.

There are hundreds if not thousands of examples of international institutions that today populate the space between the ends of the continuum in the figure, regulating everything from bank settlements to communications protocols to orbital slots for satellites to food safety to environmental and consumer safety rules. The vast majority involve public/private collaboration in which corporations, chambers of commerce, NGOs, or other non-state actors play a direct role in formulating international rules. The reason they are not all clustered at the formal end of the continuum (as treaty organizations) is that such formal organizations are too slow, cumbersome, and inflexible to provide the rule making needed by the modern global economy.

What are we to make of this phenomenon of rapidly multiplying new forms of international or multilateral institutions? The critique of international law made by conservatives like John Bolton and, more systematically, Jeremy Rabkin centers around the excessive delegation of decision-making powers to unaccountable international bodies, powers that should properly remain under the control of constitutionally specified domestic authorities.[8] This problem exists with respect to formal institutions like the United Nations or the International Criminal Court, but it applies to an even greater degree to virtually everything on the informal side of the continuum. The only good mechanisms of political accountability and rule enforcement that exist today are the vertical silos represented by traditional states. To the extent that international rules are made not by states dealing directly with other states but rather by international organizations with poor or unclear mechanisms of accountability, or else through horizontal linkages between a hodge-podge of public and private actors, democracy has been bypassed and undermined altogether.

One could argue that since most of the new international organizations listed above deal with technical issues like standards or else with relatively noncontroversial economic issues, the problem of their democratic accountability is not important. Most people have little idea what the ISO, the Codex Alimentarius, or the International Civil Aviation Organization do and are happy to let these bodies do their work outside the glare of public scrutiny. But it should not matter whether the organization's domain is obscure if it is violating an important principle of democratic accountability; moreover, many of the issues that these bodies deal with are increasingly political.

The ISO, for example, has been moving from its traditional concern with product standards to standards for services. Having developed the ISO 9000 standards for quality assurance in the 1980s, it moved on in the 1990s to the issue of environmental certification under ISO 14000. Environmental rules are not simply technical; they involve major political disputes between European and American companies and interest groups regarding when and how certification should be given. Similarly, the seemingly technical issue of food safety overseen by the Food and Agriculture Program's Codex Alimentarius has become intensely politicized as a result of European/American controversies over the safety of genetically modified foods.[9]

The point of this discussion is not to argue the rights and wrongs of particular decisions and organizations but simply to point out that the world of multi-multilateralism already exists. International cooperation today occurs under the guidance of new institutional forms that do not correspond to the traditional model of formal treaty organizations created by sovereign states.

It is not an accident that these new organizational forms have emerged initially to foster technical and economic cooperation, because the needs of global business have dictated that decisions be made efficiently. Formal organizations acting on the basis of instructions that come up the accountability channels of sovereign states are too inefficient to suit the economic needs of the global economy. We have accepted a tradeoff of legitimacy, transparency, and accountability for the sake of efficient decision making in the economic realm; the difficult question is exactly how the competing goals of legitimacy and effectiveness should be balanced.

A recent example of this need for balance concerns the way that domain names are allocated on the Internet. The Internet Corporation for Assigned Names and Numbers (ICANN) was established by the Clinton administration in 1998 as a private, nonprofit corporation, incorporated in California, to take over the function of assigning and regulating so-called top-level domains (suffixes like ".com" or ".org") for the Commerce Department, which owned the root server that contained the master directory of all Internet addresses. ICANN's structure was peculiar for an organization that was performing an official regulatory function and, indeed, an international regulatory role. It initially had a five-member board composed of information technology (IT) industry insiders, with nontransparent and unaccountable mechanisms for taking public input, not just from non-Americans but from U.S. citizens as well.[10]

The reason ICANN was created in this fashion was that most American IT industry professionals believed that the existing global regulator that normally should have taken responsibility for this function, the International Telecommunications Union (ITU), was hopelessly slow-moving and bureaucratic. The ITU is one of the world's oldest international public unions; it was founded in 1865 and thus predates the United Nations by almost a century. It is a formal treaty organization that sets international telecommunications tariffs and standards on the basis of negotiations between its member states. ICANN, on the other hand, was modeled on the Internet Engineering Task Force (IETF), which had developed the communications protocols without which the Internet could not function. ICANN had the loose, informal structure of many of the California companies that participated in the IETF and sought to duplicate the latter's rapid, bottom-up decision-making style.[11]

The only problem with ICANN, as it turned out, was that whatever its virtues in terms of efficient decision making, it came to be regarded as totally illegitimate by many of the Internet's important stakeholders, especially non-Americans, who had no idea of how this body was making decisions that ultimately affected them. The legal scholar Michael Froomkin believes that ICANN was both illegal and unconstitutional because it was a regulatory body that should have been subject, like all U.S. regulators, to the 1946 Administrative Procedure Act, which lays out formal requirements for transparency and accountability.[12]

ICANN's legitimacy crisis is such that by 2005 there were widespread calls to disband it altogether and to return its functions to the ITU. This is ironic in that this switch would surrender a huge amount of efficiency for the perceived legitimacy of the formal body.

The preceding discussion of obscure bodies like the ISO or ICANN may not seem relevant to the emotional disputes that emerged before the Iraq war over multilateralism and international legitimacy. But they are part of the same problem: on the one hand, formal international organizations perceived to be legitimate, whether the U.N. Security Council or the ITU, are hopelessly inefficient, while efficient forms of international cooperation, from coalitions of the willing to ICANN, are not perceived to be legitimate. Efficient decision making inevitably requires delegation, yet it is precisely delegation that causes problems of legitimacy.

It is very hard to develop a principled position on how this tradeoff should be made. People on the left by and large demand formal accountability of the United States when it decides to intervene militarily, but are happy to accept the results of an informal negotiation of a corporate code of conduct when it is the only way to constrain the behavior of a multinational corporation. Conservatives, on the other hand, are distrustful of the unaccountable nature of NGOs and the informal, participatory institutions that have grown up around them. But they are supportive of loosely structured and largely nonaccountable institutions that facilitate the workings of the global economy. And they are certainly not willing to concede the need for formal accountability when it comes to security-related decision making.

In the security realm, multi-multilateralism may be one approach to resolving the collective-action problem revealed by the Iraq war. Since the United Nations will continue to have limitations in its ability to deal with serious threats to international security like rogue states with WMD or conflicts requiring muscular peace enforcement, a multiplicity of geographically and functionally overlapping institutions will permit the United States and other powers to "forum shop" for an appropriate instrument to facilitate international cooperation. This happened during the Kosovo conflict: when a Russian veto in the Security Council made it impossible for the United Nations to act, the United States and its European allies shifted the venue to NATO, where the Russians were not members. The NATO alliance, while operationally cumbersome, provided legitimacy for military intervention in a way that the United Nations could not.

Indeed, NATO itself could get a second wind as a security organization in the wake of the collapse of the drive toward a European constitution. The Euro-Gaullists have traditionally downplayed NATO in favor of the European Union and hoped that the latter would become a unified counterweight to American influence. But the striking "no" votes by France and Holland in mid-2005 rejecting the European constitution have put the further deepening of Europe on indefinite hold. The publics in these two core European countries seemed to be telling the political elites that they preferred a looser union based on national sovereignty and diversity within the European Union. This opens up new possibilities for reinvigorating the NATO alliance.

NATO has fewer legitimacy problems than the United Nations. All its members are genuine liberal democracies, and all share important core values and institutions. It is a body where the United States has a great many friends, particularly since it was expanded to include the new democracies of Eastern Europe. It is also a body from which Washington's chief critic, France, has largely excluded itself, and where Russian and Chinese vetoes do not apply. Since NATO operates by consensus, it sacrifices a great deal of efficacy in decision making. As noted earlier, the cumbersomeness of the NATO machinery in the Kosovo war was one of the reasons why some members of the Bush administration opted for unilateralism. But NATO nonetheless has played an important role in supporting recent U.S. objectives in Afghanistan and Darfur.

Many neoconservatives after the Iraq war insisted that they weren't unilateralists out of principle; when asked to name a multilateral organization they liked, they would point to NATO. But they weren't serious about this: when NATO proved unwilling to support the Bush administration over Iraq, they rejected NATO as well. Being willing to work within a multilateral framework does not mean accepting support only on your terms; that is just another form of unilateralism.

If the United States seriously committed itself to acting in the future through the NATO alliance, it would trade freedom of action for legitimacy. NATO supported the Afghan intervention but not the invasion of Iraq. Had the United States submitted itself not to a "global test" but to a test involving most of the world's developed democracies, it would not have launched the second war and in the end would have been better off for having observed that self-restraint. It is not a bad habit of mind for policy makers in Washington to feel they have to be able to sway opinion in this key group of countries.

In return for accepting this kind of constraint on its freedom of action, the United States could reasonably demand a streamlining of NATO's decision-making machinery. NATO in peacetime runs by consensus, and in Kosovo the need to get all its member nations to agree on lists of bombing targets was extremely cumbersome. Now that NATO has twenty-six members, it is reasonable to seek a different type of decision-making process, based on weighted votes or delegation to a smaller executive committee.

There is room for considerable creativity in designing other new multilateral security organizations. East Asian security, for example, has been based since the end of the Second World War on a bilateral hub-and-spoke system of alliances centered on Washington. Cold War bipolarity has given way, however, to a more complex situation: North Korea has become the chief short-term regional security threat; China presents a long-term danger but can be helpful with Korea now; South Korea has moved toward North Korea and away from the United States; and Japan seeks to use the U.S. alliance to balance China and North Korea. At the same time, new regional multilateral institutions like ASEAN Plus Three and the East Asian Summit have emerged that do not include the United States. There are more possibilities for new alignments and new institutions than at any time since the 1950s.

The basic strategic choice here is whether any new political structures should include China. It would be possible, for example, to turn the Six Party Talks on North Korea's nuclear program into a permanent five-power organization to provide a forum for discussing regional security issues similar to the Organization for Security and Cooperation in Europe (OSCE).[13] Alternatively, it would be possible to start building a coalition of democratic states in East Asia that would initially include the United States, Japan, Australia, New Zealand, and perhaps India, first as an integrated economic zone and perhaps later as a fledgling security pact. At the present juncture, Japan would not favor a new multilateral organization that included China, while most of the ASEAN countries would oppose a free-trade area that excluded it. In a multi-multilateral world, the United States might seek to create both institutions, one that included China and one that did not. The first would seek to accommodate China and recognize its growing influence in the region; the second would be a hedge against the possibility that China might turn overtly aggressive.

Many Americans have rightly criticized the United Nations for including many nondemocracies and for becoming a platform by which nondemocratic states can hypocritically attack the United States and other genuine democracies like Israel for a variety of alleged abuses. This criticism suggests that the world needs an alliance of democratic states that would be similar in conception to the original League of Nations envisioned by Immanuel Kant. (Kant's league, unlike the eventual League of Nations or the United Nations, required that its members have a republican form of government.) NATO is one such organization, but it includes democracies only in Europe and North America.

A broader organization of democracies actually exists, in the form of a group called the Community of Democracies, founded in Warsaw in 2000 with backing from the Clinton administration. Its members include many of the new Third Wave democracies in Eastern Europe, Latin America, and East Asia that underwent democratic transitions since the 1970s. Since then, however, the Community of Democracies has been virtually invisible: without a permanent staff or secretariat, the organization has been kept alive but has no clear sense of mission or accomplishment. The Community of Democracies could develop its own democracy-promotion mission, providing election monitors, training, or other forms of support like those provided by the OSCE. But without resources and interest on the part of wealthier countries, this will not happen.

Had more attention been paid to the institutional development of the Community of Democracies, it could have played a major role in promoting Middle Eastern democracy after September 11. The Bush administration has tainted its own democracy-promotion efforts by launching the Iraq war and by its seeming unconcern with the plight of the Palestinians. While many people in the Middle East desperately want democracy for themselves, there is so much anti-Americanism in the region that they often feel the need to distance themselves from the United States and American support. Had the idea for a "broader Middle East" democracy initiative come from the Community of Democracies rather than from Washington, it might have been adopted more readily in the region.

Jeremy Rabkin has made the strong argument that global order in the twenty-first century ought to be based on the sovereignty of states, which are the only international actors that combine (at least potentially) democratic legitimacy with the ability to enforce a rule of law. In his view, international cooperation is legitimate, but it should occur only under conditions where the delegation of authority to an international body is precise and limited, and where states ultimately remain in control.[14]

This very traditional understanding of world order based on sovereignty has a lot to recommend it. As Rabkin points out, it was a doctrine originally intended to *moderate* the goals of states at the end of a prolonged period of bloody religious wars in Europe when countries sought to change the internal character of their neighbors. There are, however, a number of problems with this perspective.

First, it is incompatible with a foreign policy that seeks to improve governance and promote democracy around the world. As noted above, regime change via preventive war is not a promising method for promoting democratic change, which has to be based on internal political development. Nonetheless, the United States and other foreign countries in effect violated the sovereignty of Serbia, Georgia, and Ukraine when they supported democratic movements there with training, money, and electoral support. Respect for traditional sovereignty is a realist position and not one that is compatible with what is in the end a revolutionary American foreign policy agenda.

Second, as Stephen Krasner has pointed out, sovereignty in Rabkin's sense has been constantly violated throughout history, to the extent that he labels the idea a form of "organized hypocrisy."[15] States have not only violated the sovereignty of other states; they have voluntarily acceded to their own loss of sovereignty when it suited their purposes. The most common recent examples are developing countries that have agreed to make policy and institutional reforms in return for IMF or World Bank loans. If the ability to enforce laws within a state's territory is the sine qua non of sovereignty, then most countries in the developing world and probably many developed ones as well are not sovereign states.

As we saw in Chapter 5, state weakness and failure may be

among the most important sources of poverty in the developing world. If this is true, it implies that we are facing a huge crisis of missing sovereignty. It is fine to argue that an ideal global order should be based on a system of states, states which coherently make and enforce rules and have the capacity to deal with other states on a relatively equal basis. But we have no idea how to get most weak or failing states to meet these conditions. We can promote political development, good governance, and democracy at the margin, but for the foreseeable future there will remain a large core of states that simply do not fit the traditional sovereignty model. In dealing with failed states like Bosnia, Kosovo, Somalia, and Afghanistan, we have pretended that external actors, from the European Union to the United States to the World Bank, are overseeing a transitional arrangement before the return of full sovereignty to these places. But the prospects for actually doing so lie far down the road.

This reality has led Krasner and other observers to argue that we ought to move in the opposite direction, toward models of shared sovereignty in which states accept long-term help from the international community to provide certain basic governance services—importing good governance, in effect, from jurisdictions where it exists.[16] The most striking recent example of shared sovereignty is the Chad-Cameroon gas pipeline, in which the government of Chad agreed to put expected energy revenues from natural gas into a trust fund to be administered by the World Bank and other international trustees. Chad in effect agreed with the international community that it could not be trusted to use its own energy revenues properly and needed external help to avoid being dragged into a morass of corruption and rent-seeking.

The Chad-Cameroon pipeline was hugely controversial not only in Chad but in the rest of Africa, where many believed that it set a bad precedent for sovereignty. It is clear that if shared sovereignty is ever to become a more broadly accepted model, it will take place only under conditions where the external actor with whom governance functions are divided is regarded as legitimate. Those jurisdictions with good governance, in other words, will need to export governance to other jurisdictions that lack it. But a legitimate export regime does not currently exist and must be invented if this is to take place.

7 A Different Kind of American Foreign Policy

It seems very doubtful at this juncture that history will judge the Iraq war kindly. By invading Iraq, the Bush administration created a self-fulfilling prophecy: Iraq has now replaced Afghanistan as a magnet, training ground, and operational base for jihadist terrorists, with plenty of American targets to shoot at. The tenuous prewar connection between the Jordanian jihadist Abu Musab al-Zarqawi and the Ba'athists in Iraq has now grown into a full-scale alliance, fed by mutual resentment of the U.S. occupation. The United States still has a chance of creating a Shiite-dominated democratic Iraq, but the new government will be very weak for years to come, and heavily dependent on U.S. military support. Defense Secretary Rumsfeld, who wanted to go into Iraq with light forces and get out quickly, has as a result of this strategy bogged the U.S. military down in a long-term guerrilla war. The all-volunteer force, created in the wake of the Vietnam War, was never designed to fight protracted wars of this sort and will have difficulty sustaining recruitment and morale as time goes on. Even if the United States is able eventually to withdraw and leave behind a stable democracy, the costs will have been enormous: in the first two years after the invasion, the United States has already spent a couple of hundred billion dollars and suffered perhaps 15,000 dead and wounded. Iraqi dead as a result of the American occupation and insurgency number in the tens of thousands; although there would have been continuing abuses had Saddam Hussein been left in place, these casualties in a country we were seeking to help represent an enormous human cost. American preoccupation with Iraq limits Washington's options in other parts of the world and has distracted the attention of senior policy makers from other regions such as Asia that in the long run are likely to present greater strategic challenges.

It seems relatively clear that the Bush administration in its second term has itself sidelined regime change through preventive war in its foreign policy. In the case of the other two members of the axis of evil, Iran and North Korea, the administration has signaled that it does not intend to use military force to bring about regime change. This is in part a bow to simple reality: U.S. forces are at the moment overstretched by the continuing war in Iraq, and in any event there are no simple options for intervention to stop either the Iranian or the North Korean nuclear program. But beyond operational constraints, the administration seems to have recognized that it paid a huge political price for the Iraq war, and that preventive war cannot be the centerpiece of American strategy. Condoleezza Rice's instincts seem to be closer to Colin Powell's than to Donald Rumsfeld's, and she has far more authority with President Bush. But the ability of the administration to fix the problems it created for itself in its first four years will be limited. Repairing American credibility will not be a matter of better public relations; it will require a new team and new policies.

One of the consequences of a perceived failure in Iraq will be the discrediting of the entire neoconservative agenda and a restoration of the authority of foreign policy realists. Already there are a host of books and articles decrying America's imperial ambition and attacking the notion of trying to remake the world democratically.[1] The backlash against the neoconservative agenda may not end there. Jacksonian conservatives, those red-state Americans whose sons and daughters are the ones fighting and dying in the Middle East, aligned with the neoconservatives in support of the Iraq war. But a perceived failure of the policy may push them back toward a more isolationist foreign policy, which is a more natural political position for them in any case.

It would be too bad if this backlash occurred, and the United States went through another cycle of withdrawal like the one after Vietnam. The United States remains too big, wealthy, and influential for it ever to abjure big ambitions in world politics. What is needed is not a return to a narrow realism but rather a *realistic* Wilsonianism that recognizes the importance to world order of what goes on *inside* states and that better matches the available tools to the achievement of democratic ends. Such a policy would take seriously the idealistic part of the old neoconservative agenda but take a fresh look at development, international institutions, and a host of issues that conservatives, neo- and paleo-, seldom took seriously.[2]

This means, in the first instance, a dramatic demilitarization of American foreign policy and reemphasis on other types of policy instruments. Preventive war and regime change via military intervention can never be taken off the table completely, but they have to be understood as very extreme measures. It is not enough to say "we can't afford to wait" in dealing with rogue states because we seldom have simple, clean options for using force. The *National Security Strategy of the United States* ought to be officially revised to provide clear criteria for when we believe preventive war is legitimate, and those criteria ought to be both restrictive and specific.

The rhetoric about World War IV and the global war on terrorism should cease. We are fighting hot counterinsurgency wars in Afghanistan and Iraq, and against the international jihadist movement, that we need to win. But conceiving the larger struggle as a global war comparable to the world wars or the Cold War vastly overstates the scope of the problem, suggesting that we are taking on a large part of the Arab and Muslim worlds. Before the Iraq war, we were probably at war with no more than a few thousand people around the world who would consider martyring themselves and causing nihilistic damage to the United States. The scale of the problem has grown because we have unleashed a maelstrom; whatever the merits of the original intervention, walking away from Iraq now without creating a strong and stable government there will leave a festering terrorist sanctuary in the Sunni triangle. Much of the campaign against jihadist terrorism will be fought out in Western Europe by our allies; we will have little direct role in this struggle since many of the terrorists will be European citizens. Outside of combat operations in Iraq and Afghanistan, the anti-jihadist campaign will look more like a police and intelligence operation than a war.

The United States should promote both political and economic development, and it should care about what happens inside states around the world. We should do this by focusing primarily on good governance, political accountability, democracy, and strong institutions. But the primary instruments by which we do this are mostly within the realm of soft power: our ability to set an example, to train and educate, to support with advice and often money. The secret to development, whether economic or political, is that outsiders are almost never the ones who drive the process forward. It is always people within societies—sometimes a small elite, sometimes the broader civil society—who must create a demand for reform and for institutions, and who must exercise ultimate ownership over the results. This requires tremendous patience as institutions are built, organizations founded, coalitions formed, norms change, and conditions become ripe for democratic change. This process can sometimes benefit from the application of hard power, as in the Balkans, but any such application should typically be seen as an adjunct to actions by local players.

The Bush administration by the beginning of its second term had already shifted its rhetorical stance toward democracy in the Middle East substantially, moving away from an emphasis on stability and toward gentle suggestions that allies like Egypt and Saudi Arabia ought to pursue reform. Condoleezza Rice as secretary of state has stated fairly clearly that the administration is willing to take the risks of having extremists come to power in open elections.[3] This is a welcome change, but it is important that we be clear in our own minds why we are making it.

Democratizing the Middle East is something that is desirable in its own right, *and not because it will solve our problem with terrorism.* If Olivier Roy's analysis of the sources of jihadism is correct, an important part of the terrorist problem lies in Western Europe, not the Middle East, and is a by-product of immigration, globalization, and other characteristics of a part of the world that is already open and democratic. Even if Egypt and Saudi Arabia turned into stable democracies overnight, we would still have a deeply embedded terrorism problem for years to come.

Moreover, we should not kid ourselves about the likely short-term costs of Middle Eastern democracy. A Turkish-style transition to a secular democracy based on Western models is extremely unlikely in most parts of the Arab world. Greater democracy will come through political participation of Islamist groups in a pluralist political order. Many of these groups have an uncertain commitment to democracy. Although many will want to take part in elections, most are not liberal at all, and some, like Hamas in Gaza or Hizbollah in Lebanon, are terrorist organizations. What we can hope for is that they will eventually evolve into more responsible political parties willing to accept pluralism in principle rather than simply out of necessity. But what may emerge in the short run may seem pretty unappealing if you care about women's rights, religious tolerance, and the like.[4]

Although political reform in the Arab world is desirable, the United States faces a big short-run problem: it has virtually no credibility or moral authority in the region. The dominant image of the United States is not the Statue of Liberty but the photographs of prisoner abuse at Abu Ghraib; pro-Western liberal reformers feel they have to distance themselves from the United States and are targeted for accepting grants from organizations like the National Endowment for Democracy. It is to be hoped that this will not be a permanent situation, but it could mean that a strong push for political change coming from Washington at this juncture would be counterproductive. This difficulty underlines the importance of having alternative international institutions that can distance themselves a bit from Washington, such as the Community of Democracies, to promote democracy and reform.

What the Bush administration and its neoconservative supporters failed to appreciate before the Iraq war was the fact that
the kind of lopsidedly unipolar world that emerged after the
Cold War had stoked broad new currents of anti-Americanism.
Signs of this were clearly evident well before the 2000 election.
What recognition of this fact should have led the administration
to do was not to abjure the use of American power but to be more
cautious in it, to use soft rather than hard power, and to devise
more subtle and indirect ways of shaping the world.

American power remains critical to world order; the United
States is not just a giant version of Sweden or Switzerland on the
world stage. But American power is often the most effective when
it is not seen. U.S. forces in East Asia and the U.S.-Japanese alliance permit Japan to maintain a relatively weak military establishment, thereby avoiding remilitarization that would be threatening to China, Korea, and other states in Asia. By having large
forces, and more important, the technology, mobility, and logis-
tical networks that allow them to be deployed around the world,
the United States discourages middle-range powers from seeking to militarily dominate their regions.

American power is often more useful when it is latent. Despite
the fact that the United States spends roughly as much on its
military as the rest of the world put together, the Iraq war has
demonstrated that there are clear limits to the U.S. military's effectiveness. It is not well configured for fighting prolonged insurgencies; the strains of the Iraq war have already forced the

Pentagon in the Bush administration's second-term Quadrennial Review to question the ability of the United States to fight two simultaneous regional wars.

The historical model that we ought to consider for the exercise of American power in today's unipolar world is not Henry Kissinger's favorite, the realist Austrian prince Metternich, but the German chancellor Otto von Bismarck. Bismarck launched two wars, against Austria and France, to unify Germany and secure a dominant position in central Europe. After this had been achieved by 1871, however, he understood that Germany's main task would be to reassure its intimidated and resentful neighbors that Germany had become a status quo power. His clear goal was to prevent the formation of hostile coalitions that would openly seek to oppose German power. His diplomacy after 1871 achieved this brilliantly through the Reinsurance Treaty, the Berlin Conference, and a host of other initiatives designed to soften the face of new German power. His successors, however, did not have the same clear understanding of the need to reassure rather than intimidate, and did foolish things like building a large blue-water navy. The result was formation of the French-Russian-British Entente, which set the stage for the First World War.

The United States is not going to provoke France and Germany into forming a hostile military coalition, but it has provoked a great deal of unity among normally fractious Europeans around the view that the irresponsible exercise of American power is one of the chief problems in contemporary politics. This has already resulted in "soft balancing," where countries like Germany and France have tried to block American initiatives or refused cooperation when asked for it.[5] Similarly, Asian countries have been busy building regional multilateral organizations because Washington has been perceived as not particularly interested in their needs. Hugo Chavez in Venezuela has been using oil revenues to detach countries in the Andes and Caribbean from the American orbit, while Russia and China are collaborating to slowly push the United States out of Central Asia.

The United States cannot avoid provoking fear and resentment given its de facto power any more than Bismarck's Germany could, but it can try to minimize the backlash by deliberately seeking ways to downplay its dominance. The Bush administration did nearly the opposite: it launched not one but two wars in response to September 11 in the belief that it would somehow not be regarded as credible if it did not "make a statement" beyond the Afghan intervention; it announced an open-ended doctrine of regime change and preventive war; it withdrew from or criticized a series of international institutions; and it implicitly asserted a principle of American exceptionalism in its self-proclaimed benevolent ordering of the world.

The most important way that American power can be exercised at this juncture is not through the exercise of military power but through the ability of the United States to shape international institutions. John Ikenberry has argued that this was precisely the way that the United States exercised its then-dominant power in the years immediately following World War II.[6] The neoconservatives had a true insight that American ideals and self-interests are often aligned, but they failed to understand that that alignment most often occurred through America's ability to create durable political frameworks through which it could achieve long-term cooperation with like-minded nations. The deficit of workable international institutions is plainly evident in the wake of the Iraq war.

Realistic institutions for world order in the post–September 11 period require two things that are often mutually inconsistent: power and legitimacy. Power is needed to deal with threats not just from rogue states but from the new non-state actors that may in the future employ weapons of mass destruction. It must be capable of being deployed quickly and decisively; its use will in some cases require the violation of national sovereignty and may in some cases require preemption.

International legitimacy, on the other hand, requires working through international institutions that are inherently slow-moving, rigid, and hobbled by cumbersome procedures and methods. Legitimacy is ultimately based on consent, which is in turn a by-product of a slow process of diplomacy and persuasion. International institutions exist in part to reduce the transaction costs of achieving consent, but under the best of circumstances they necessarily move less quickly than security requires.

It is doubtful whether we will ever be able to create truly democratic global institutions, particularly if they aspire, like the United Nations, to be globally representative. The European Union has been seeking to create a democratic supranational entity on a continent that by and large shares a common culture and history, and it has run into massive obstacles with regard to both legitimacy and effectiveness as it grows.

On the other hand, if true democracy, with all its institutions of elections, courts, executive authority, and separated powers, seems hard to obtain on an international scale, a more modest goal of democratic accountability may be within reach. The reason for thinking so is simply that, after the end of the Cold War, a much larger number of countries are democratic than were previously. Although international cooperation will have to be based on sovereign states for the foreseeable future, shared ideas of legitimacy and human rights will weaken objections that the United States should not be accountable to regimes that are not themselves accountable.

One might ask why the United States should want to bind itself unnecessarily when it is at the peak of its power relative to the rest of the international system. International institutions are for the Lilliputians of the world, who have no other way of tying down Gulliver. America is sovereign, not just over its own territory but over much of the world; why change?[7] This was, of course, the question that the Athenians put to the Melians in Thucydides' famous dialogue.

One answer has to do with American beliefs. The French writer Pierre Hassner—who was, incidentally, once a student of Leo Strauss—observed that in their domestic institutions, Americans believe in checks and balances because they distrust concentrated power, even if well-intentioned and democratically legitimated.[8] But in the unipolar post–Cold War world, he argues, they have uncritically promoted U.S. hegemony and said to the rest of the world, "Trust me." If unchecked power is corrupting in a domestic context, why would it not also be bad for the power-holder internationally?

One could argue that the Bush administration's mistakes in its first term were prudential, not errors of principle. It understood well that the United States could not avoid exercising power and taking risks in the face of unusual challenges; it just had the bad luck to roll snake eyes rather than sevens or elevens. Whether these mistakes were simply bad luck and excusable in light of the extraordinary circumstances following upon the September 11 attacks, or whether they reflected a fixed mind-set and unjustifiable self-confidence will be up to each individual to judge.

But the fact that these errors were made by the world's sole superpower exposes the fatal flaw lying at the heart of a world order based on American benevolent hegemony. The hegemon has to be not just well-intentioned but also prudent and smart in its exercise of power. It was not Condoleezza Rice but Bill Clinton's secretary of state Madeleine Albright who once asserted that Americans deserve to lead because they can "see further" than other people. If this were consistently true and widely acknowledged, the world would still only grudgingly concede primacy to American judgment and wishes. If American judgment turns out to be more shortsighted than that of others, then our unipolar world is in for a rough ride.

Notes

Chapter 1: Principles and Prudence

1. The administration's decision was indicated in the so-called Downing Street memo, written by Matthew Rycroft, an aide to British Prime Minister Tony Blair's foreign policy advisor David Manning, on July 23, 2002, after a visit to Washington to consult with the Bush administration.

2. Walter Russell Mead, "The Jacksonian Tradition and American Foreign Policy," *National Interest* 58 (1999): 5–29.

Chapter 2: The Neoconservative Legacy

1. Elizabeth Drew, quoted in Joshua Muravchik, "The Neoconservative Cabal," and Howard Dean, quoted in Adam Wolfson, "Conservatives and Neoconservatives," in Irwin Stelzer, ed., *The Neocon Reader* (New York: Grove Press, 2005), 243, 216; Mary Wakefield, *The Daily Telegraph*, Jan. 9, 2004.

2. See David Brooks, "The Neocon Cabal and Other Fantasies," and Max Boot, "Myths About Neoconservatism," in Stelzer, *Neocon Reader*.

3. See Irving Kristol, <i>Reflections of a Neoconservative: Looking Back, Looking Ahead</i> (New York: Basic, 1983); Kristol, <i>Neoconservatism: The Autobiography of an Idea</i> (New York: Free Press, 1995); and Norman Podhoretz, "Neoconservatism: A Eulogy," in Norman Podhoretz, <i>The Norman Podhoretz Reader</i> (New York: Free Press, 2004).

4. Alain Frachon and Daniel Vernet, <i>L'Amérique messianique</i> (Paris: Editions de Seuil, 2004); James Mann, <i>The Rise of the Vulcans: The History of Bush's War Cabinet</i> (New York: Viking, 2004); Murray Friedman, <i>Jewish Intellectuals and the Shaping of Public Policy</i> (New York: Cambridge University Press, 2005); see, inter alia, Stefan Halper and Jonathan Clark, <i>America Alone: The Neo-Conservatives and the Global Order</i> (Cambridge: Cambridge University Press, 2004).

5. Joseph Dorman, <i>Arguing the World: New York Intellectuals in Their Own Words</i> (Chicago: University of Chicago Press, 2001).

6. See Norman Podhoretz, <i>Breaking Ranks: A Political Memoir</i> (New York: Harper and Row, 1979), <i>Ex-Friends</i> (New York: Free Press, 1999), and <i>My Love Affair with America</i> (New York: Free Press, 2000).

7. Nathan Glazer, <i>Affirmative Discrimination</i> (New York: Basic, 1975); James Q. Wilson, <i>Thinking About Crime</i> (New York: Basic, 1975); Wilson and Richard Herrnstein, <i>Crime and Human Nature</i> (New York: Simon and Schuster, 1985); Wilson, <i>Varieties of Police Behavior: The Management of Law and Order in Eight Communities</i> (Cambridge: Harvard University Press, 1968); James Q. Wilson and George Kelling, "Broken Windows: The Police and Neighborhood Safety," <i>Atlantic Monthly</i> (March 1982): 29–38.

8. Daniel P. Moynihan, <i>The Negro Family: A Case for National Action</i> (Washington, D.C.: U.S. Department of Labor, 1965); Charles Murray, <i>Losing Ground</i> (New York: Basic, 1984). Many of the premises of Murray's critique of AFDC were accepted by analysts on the Left. See William Julius Wilson, <i>The Truly Disadvantaged: The Inner City, the Underclass, and Public Policy</i> (Chicago: University of Chicago Press, 1988).

9. Mark Lilla, "Leo Strauss: The European," *New York Review of Books*, Oct. 21, 2004; Lilla, "The Closing of the Straussian Mind," *New York Review of Books*, Nov. 4, 2004; Anne Norton, *Leo Strauss and the Politics of American Empire* (New Haven: Yale University Press, 2004); Shadia B. Drury, *The Political Ideas of Leo Strauss* (New York: St. Martin's, 1988). Drury is the source of the idea that Strauss promotes "noble lies" by public officials. See Danny Postel, "Noble Lies and Perpetual War: Leo Strauss, the Neocons, and Iraq," OpenDemocracy.com, Oct. 16, 2003. For a rebuttal, see Mark Blitz, "Leo Strauss, the Strauss-ians and American Foreign Policy," OpenDemocracy.com, Nov. 13, 2003. Lyndon LaRouche, commercial, WTOP Radio, Washington, D.C., 2004.

10. Harry V. Jaffa, *Crisis of the House Divided: An Interpretation of the Lincoln-Douglas Debates* (Seattle: University of Washington Press, 1959). These themes are continued in his later *A New Birth of Freedom: Abraham Lincoln and the Coming of the Civil War* (Lanham, Md.: Rowman and Littlefield, 2000). See also Lilla, "Closing of the Straussian Mind."

11. The lecture that eventually became the article "The End of History?" was originally given at Bloom's John M. Olin Center at the University of Chicago on Feb. 8, 1989, in the context of a series entitled "The Decline of the West?" Allan Bloom, *The Closing of the American Mind* (New York: Simon and Schuster, 1987).

12. Plato, *Republic,* trans. Allan Bloom (New York: Basic Books, 1968), 561c–d.

13. Leo Strauss, *Natural Right and History* (Chicago: University of Chicago Press, 1953), 294–323, esp. 314–16. On the founding fathers see, for example, David F. Epstein, *The Political Theory of the Federalist* (Chicago: University of Chicago Press, 1984).

14. Adam Wolfson, "Conservatives and Neoconservatives," 225.

15. The single most important decision that MacArthur made as Supreme Commander of the Allied Powers in Tokyo was to retain the Japanese

emperor. It is perhaps not an accident that MacArthur lived in East Asia almost continuously from the time he helped establish the Philippine Army in the 1930s until his recall by President Truman during the Korean War.

16. See Francis Fukuyama, "The March of Equality," *Journal of Democracy* 11, no. 1 (2000): 11–17.

17. Albert Wohlstetter, Henry S. Rowen, et al., *Selection and Use of Strategic Air Bases* (Santa Monica, Calif.: Rand Corporation, R-266, 1954). A shorter version was published as "The Delicate Balance of Terror" in *Foreign Affairs* 27, no. 2 (Jan. 1959).

18. Henry A. Kissinger, *A World Restored: Europe After Napoleon* (Gloucester, Mass.: Peter Smith, 1973); Kissinger, *Diplomacy* (New York: Simon and Schuster, 1994).

19. This was true of Strauss's students as well; it is even harder to extract an economic ideology from his writings than a political one.

20. See Wolfson, "Conservatives and Neoconservatives."

21. Boot, "Myths About Neoconservatism."

22. William Kristol and Robert Kagan, "Toward a Neo-Reaganite Foreign Policy," *Foreign Affairs* 75, no. 4 (1996): 18–32; Kristol and Kagan, *Present Dangers: Crisis and Opportunity in American Foreign and Defense Policy* (San Francisco: Encounter, 2000); Jeane Kirkpatrick, "A Normal Country in a Normal Time," *National Interest* (Fall 1990): 40–44; Kristol and Kagan, *Present Dangers*, 12.

23. Boot, "Myths About Neoconservatism."

24. See Robert Kagan, "America's Crisis of Legitimacy," *Foreign Affairs* 83, no. 2 (2004): 65–87, and the subsequent debate between him and Robert W. Tucker and David C. Hendrickson; Tucker and Hendrickson, "The Sources of American Legitimacy," *Foreign Affairs* 83, no. 6 (2004); and Kagan, "A Matter of Record," *Foreign Affairs* 84, no. 1 (2005); Kristol and Kagan, *Present Dangers*, 16–17.

25. David Brooks, "A Return to National Greatness," *Weekly Standard*, Mar. 3, 1997.

26. On neoconservative issues see Francis Fukuyama, "The National Prospect Symposium Contribution," *Commentary* 100, no. 5 (1995): 55–56. On economics see, for example, Daniel Bell, *The Cultural Contradictions of Capitalism* (New York: Basic, 1976), and Irving Kristol, *Two Cheers for Capitalism* (New York: Basic, 1978). That neoconservative treatments of economics tended toward orthodoxy was not universally true; for an interesting critique of neoclassical economics from a Straussian point of view, see Steven E. Rhoads, *The Economist's View of the World: Government, Markets, and Public Policy* (Cambridge: Cambridge University Press, 1985).

27. See Kiron Skinner, ed., *Reagan: A Life in Letters* (New York: Free Press, 2003). Later on, of course, Reagan recognized the reality of the changes brought about by Mikhail Gorbachev and negotiated with him actively.

28. This was in his speech at the American Enterprise Institute, Feb. 26, 2003.

29. For a comprehensive realist critique of international institutions, see John J. Mearsheimer, "The False Promise of International Institutions," *International Security* 19, no. 3 (1994): 5–49. On multilateral cooperation see Boot, "Myths About Neoconservatism."

30. Stephen Sestanovich, "American Maximalism," *National Interest* 79 (Spring 2005): 13–23.

31. See Michael Mandelbaum, "Coup de Grace: The End of the Soviet Union," *Foreign Affairs* 71, no. 1 (1991): 164–83, and *The Dawn of Peace in Europe* (New York: Twentieth Century Fund, 1996).

32. In 1989 many Soviet observers believed that Yegor Ligachev represented the hard-liners in Gorbachev's Politburo and imagined that there was an active debate in the Kremlin on whether to intervene

militarily in Poland, Hungary, and East Germany as these countries moved away from Moscow. I had the remarkable experience of meeting Ligachev in Washington a few years later, when he explained that military intervention had never crossed the minds of anyone in the Politburo.

33. For both a restatement of the argument in *The End of History and the Last Man* and an analysis of what I regard as the most salient critiques of it, see the preface to the second paperback edition (New York: Free Press, 2006).

34. Kenneth Jowitt, "Rage, Hubris, and Regime Change: The Urge to Speed History Along," *Policy Review* 118 (April–May 2003): 33–42.

35. Kristol and Kagan, *Present Dangers*, 20.

36. See Fareed Zakaria, *The Future of Freedom: Illiberal Democracy at Home and Abroad* (New York: Norton, 2003); Thomas Carothers, "The End of the Transition Paradigm," *Journal of Democracy* 13, no. 1 (2002): 5–21.

37. G. John Ikenberry and Daniel Deudney, "The International Sources of Soviet Change," *International Security* 16, no. 3 (1991): 74–118.

38. For an example, see Donald Kagan and Frederick W. Kagan, "Peace for Our Time?" *Commentary* 110, no. 2 (Sept. 2000): 42–47.

Chapter 3: Threat, Risk, and Preventive War

1. Paul R. Pillar, *Terrorism and U.S. Foreign Policy* (Washington, D.C.: Brookings Institution, 2001); Graham T. Allison, Jr., *Nuclear Terrorism: The Ultimate Preventable Catastrophe* (New York: Times Books, 2004). For an argument that September 11 represented a unique case rather than the beginning of a long-term trend, see John Mueller, "Harbinger or Aberration? A 9/11 Provocation," *National Interest* 69 (Fall 2002): 45–50.

2. See Norman Podhoretz, "World War IV: How It Started, What It Means, and Why We Have to Win," *Commentary* 118, no. 2 (2004):

17–54; Charles Krauthammer, "In Defense of Democratic Realism," *National Interest* 77 (Fall 2004).

3. Gilles Kepel, *The War for Muslim Minds: Islam and the West* (Cambridge: Belknap, 2004); Olivier Roy, *The Failure of Political Islam* (Cambridge: Harvard University Press, 1996). See also Olivier Roy, *Globalized Islam: The Search for a New Ummah* (New York: Columbia University Press, 2004).

4. Roy, *Globalized Islam*, chap. 1.

5. Ladan Boroumand and Roya Boroumand, "Terror, Islam, and Democracy," *Journal of Democracy* 13, no. 2 (2002): 5–20. That jihadism is a syncretism of Western beliefs is also the essence of Olivier Roy's characterization of Islamism.

6. This argument is made more fully in Francis Fukuyama and Nadav Samin, "Can Any Good Come of Radical Islam?" *Commentary* 114, no. 2 (2002): 34–38.

7. In 2005, Mali assumed chairmanship of the Community of Democracies.

8. Among the older group of respondents, 51 percent expressed a desire to emigrate from their home countries. Of these, 46 percent wanted to emigrate to Western Europe and 36 percent to the United States or Canada. Among younger respondents, 45 percent wanted to emigrate, with 45 percent wanting to go to North America (UNDP, Arab Human Development Report, 2002, 30).

9. Max Boot, "Exploiting the Palestinians: Everyone's Doing It," *Weekly Standard*, Jan. 28, 2003; Barry Rubin, "The Real Roots of Arab Anti-Americanism," *Foreign Affairs* 81, no. 6 (2002): 73–85.

10. *National Security Strategy of the United States* (Washington, D.C.: U.S. Government Printing Office, 2002).

11. Cover letter to the *National Security Strategy*. This echoes language in the speech given by President Bush at West Point in June 2002 in which he stated: "For much of the last century, America's defense re-

lied on the Cold War doctrines of deterrence and containment. In some cases, those strategies still apply. But new threats also require new thinking. Deterrence—the promise of massive retaliation against nations—means nothing against shadowy terrorist networks with no nation or citizens to defend. Containment is not possible when unbalanced dictators with weapons of mass destruction can deliver those weapons on missiles or secretly provide them to terrorist allies. . . . If we wait for threats to fully materialize, we will have waited too long. . . . We must take the battle to the enemy, disrupt his plans, and confront the worst threats before they emerge" ("Remarks by the President at 2002 Graduation Exercise of the United States Military Academy," West Point, N.Y., June 1, 2002).

12. John Lewis Gaddis, *Surprise, Security, and the American Experience* (Cambridge: Harvard University Press, 2004).

13. For a discussion, see John Lewis Gaddis, "Grand Strategy in the Second Term," *Foreign Affairs* 84, no. 1 (2005): 2–15.

14. *A More Secure World: Our Shared Responsibility.* Report of the Secretary-General's High-Level Panel on Threats, Challenges, and Change (New York: United Nations, 2004), 63–64.

15. Of course, this outcome was itself dependent on Saddam Hussein's poor judgment; had he waited until he had a nuclear weapon before invading Kuwait, he might still be ruler of that country today.

16. Anthony Eden, *Full Circle: The Memoirs of Anthony Eden* (Boston: Houghton Mifflin, 1960); Jack Snyder, *The Ideology of the Offensive: Military Decision Making and the Disaster* (Ithaca: Cornell University Press, 1984); Richard K. Betts, "Suicide from Fear of Death?" *Foreign Affairs* 82, no. 1 (2003): 34–43.

17. Kenneth Jowitt, "Rage, Hubris, and Regime Change: The Urge to Speed History Along," *Policy Review* 118 (April–May 2003): 33–42.

18. Roberta Wohlstetter, *Pearl Harbor: Warning and Decision* (Stanford: Stanford University Press, 1965).

19. President Bush added: "Saddam Hussein is harboring terrorists and the instruments of terror, the instruments of mass death and destruction. And he cannot be trusted. The risk is simply too great that he will use them, or provide them to a terror network" (speech in Cincinnati, Oct. 8, 2002).

20. Laurie Mylroie, *Study of Revenge: Saddam Hussein's Unfinished War* (Washington, D.C.: AEI Press, 2000); Stephen F. Hayes, *The Connection: How al Qaeda's Collaboration with Saddam Hussein Has Endangered America* (New York: HarperCollins, 2004); Kenneth M. Pollack, *The Threatening Storm: The Case for Invading Iraq* (New York: Random House, 2002).

21. By her own contention, Mylroie's case that Ramzi Yousef, the man convicted of the 1993 World Trade Center bombing, was an Iraqi intelligence agent could be shown to be false if one could prove that he and Abdul Bassit (from whom he allegedly stole his identity) were the same height. To date, no evidence has been produced that they were different people.

22. The presidential commission on prewar intelligence concerning Iraq has indicated that our knowledge of the Iranian and North Korean programs is not much better than it was for Iraq's. See *The Commission on the Intelligence Capabilities of the United States Regarding Weapons of Mass Destruction, Report to the President of the United States* (Washington, D.C.: U.S. Government Printing Office, Mar. 31, 2005).

23. *Comprehensive Report of the Special Advisor to the DCI on Iraq's WMD* (Washington, D.C.: Central Intelligence Agency, Sept. 30, 2004).

Chapter 4: American Exceptionalism and International Legitimacy

1. See Paul D. Wolfowitz, "Clinton's First Year," *Foreign Affairs* 73, no. 1 (1994): 28–43.

2. For a reiteration of this well after the war, see the interview with Condoleezza Rice in *American Interest* 1, no. 1 (2005): 47–57.

3. This official is quoted in the preface to the paperback edition of Clark's Kosovo memoir. Clark was upset at this interpretation of his own book (Wesley K. Clark, *Waging Modern War: Bosnia, Kosovo, and the Future of Combat* [New York: Public Affairs, 2002], pp. xxvi–xxvii).

4. Stephen Sestanovich, "American Maximalism," *National Interest* 79 (Spring 2005): 13–23.

5. Mancur Olson, *The Logic of Collective Action: Public Goods and the Theory of Groups* (Cambridge: Harvard University Press, 1965).

6. During the 1991 Gulf War, both the French and the Russians kept their distance from the United States in the six-month run-up to the war. France joined the coalition only at the last minute after it had extracted a number of concessions from the Americans. It was not unreasonable to think that the French and the Russians might try to do the same in 2003. On the "European nation" see Timothy Garton Ash, *Free World: Why a Crisis of the West Reveals the Opportunity of Our Time* (London: Allen Lane, 2004), 54.

7. Charles Krauthammer, "The Unipolar Moment," *Foreign Affairs* (Winter 1990–91); see also Krauthammer, "The Unipolar Moment Revisited," *National Interest* 70 (2002): 5–20. Charles Krauthammer, "Democratic Realism: An American Foreign Policy for a Unipolar World" (Washington, D.C.: American Enterprise Institute Short Publications Series, Feb. 10, 2004).

8. William Kristol and Robert Kagan, *Present Dangers: Crisis and Opportunity in American Foreign and Defense Policy* (San Francisco: Encounter, 2000), 22.

9. Condoleezza Rice, "A Balance of Power That Favors Freedom," the 2002 Wriston Lecture at the Manhattan Institute for Policy Research, New York, Oct. 1, 2002.

10. Walter Russell Mead, *Power, Terror, Peace, and War: America's Grand Strategy in a World at Risk* (New York: Knopf, 2004).

11. These data are as of March 2004; "somewhat" to "very negative" feel-

ings about the United States were 93 percent in Jordan, 61 percent in Pakistan, 68 percent in Morocco, and 63 percent in Turkey (Pew Research Center for the People and the Press, "A Year After the Iraq War," March 16, 2004. Data available at people-press.org/reports/display.php3? ReportID=206).

12. Barlow's "Declaration of Independence of Cyberspace" begins: "Governments of the Industrial World, you weary giants of flesh and steel, I come from Cyberspace, the new home of Mind. On behalf of the future, I ask you of the past to leave us alone. You are not welcome among us. You have no sovereignty where we gather" (http://homes.eff.org/~barlow/Declaration-final.html).

13. The transistor and the integrated circuit were initially developed at Bell Labs as spin-offs of Defense Department–funded projects to develop computer systems for military purposes. Radar, jet aircraft technology, and a good deal of U.S. commercial aerospace similarly benefited from military spending. The Internet was developed by the Defense Advanced Research Projects Agency as a means of communicating after a nuclear attack.

14. Historically, the Washington Consensus developed in response to the Latin American debt crisis of the 1980s, where heavy foreign borrowing and lack of fiscal discipline led to a pathological cycle of currency crisis, devaluation, expansionary monetary policy to cover fiscal deficits, hyperinflation, and then renewed exchange rate crisis. The economic policy measures outlined in the Washington Consensus were necessary to break this cycle, and through a painful series of adjustments countries like Mexico, Brazil, and Argentina managed, by the early 1990s, to stabilize their macroeconomic balances.

15. The final story in Latin America is more complicated: while the rise of Lula in Brazil, Gutierrez in Ecuador, Vázquez in Uruguay, and Chavez in Venezuela marks a turn to the left, most of these new leaders have continued to follow relatively orthodox macroeconomic policies. Ar-

gentina's meltdown is unfairly blamed on the United States; its roots are complex and lie much more heavily in defective Argentine institutions and leadership.

16. Kishore Mahbubani, *Beyond the Age of Innocence: Rebuilding Trust Between America and the World* (New York: Public Affairs, 2005), chap. 1.

Chapter 5: Social Engineering and the Problem of Development

1. James Q. Wilson has been consistently skeptical about the chances for democracy promotion, both generally and in Iraq. See his article "Democracy for All?" in *Commentary* 107, no. 3 (2000).

2. Rick Atkinson, *In the Company of Soldiers: A Chronicle of Combat* (New York: Henry Holt and Co., 2004); Tim Russert, interview with Vice President Dick Cheney, *Meet the Press*, NBC News, Mar. 16, 2003.

3. See Adam Garfinkle, "The Impossible Imperative? Conjuring Arab Democracy," *National Interest* 69 (Fall 2002): 156–67; *President Discusses the Future of Iraq*, Speech to the American Enterprise Institute, Washington, D.C., Feb. 26, 2003. As noted earlier, the long trend toward the spread of liberal democracy is the central theme of my book *The End of History and the Last Man* (New York: Free Press, 1992).

4. William Kristol and Robert Kagan, *Present Dangers: Crisis and Opportunity in American Foreign and Defense Policy* (San Francisco: Encounter, 2000), 14–17.

5. For a description of these models, see Kaushik Basu, *Analytical Development Economics: The Less Developed Economy Revisited* (Cambridge: MIT Press, 1997).

6. See David Ekbladh, "From Consensus to Crisis: The Postwar Career of Nation Building in U.S. Foreign Relations," and Frank Sutton, "Nation-Building in the Heyday of the Classic Development Ideology: Ford Foundation Experience in the 1950s and 1960s," in Francis Fukuyama, ed., *Nation-Building: Beyond Afghanistan and Iraq* (Baltimore: Johns Hopkins University Press, 2006).

7. William R. Easterly, *The Elusive Quest for Growth: Economists' Adventures and Misadventures in the Tropics* (Cambridge: MIT Press, 2001).

8. Ruth Levine et al., *Millions Saved: Proven Successes in Global Health* (Washington, D.C.: Center for Global Development, 2004).

9. Walt Whitman Rostow, *The Stages of Economic Growth: A Non-Communist Manifesto* (Cambridge: Cambridge University Press, 1960).

10. See Nicolas van de Walle, *African Economies and the Politics of Permanent Crisis, 1979–1999* (Cambridge: Cambridge University Press, 2001).

11. For an analysis of state weakness and failure in Africa, see Crawford Young, *The African Colonial State in Comparative Perspective* (New Haven: Yale University Press, 1997), Jeffery Herbst, *States and Power in Africa* (Princeton: Princeton University Press, 2000), and William Reno, *Warlord Politics and African States* (Boulder, Colo.: Lynne Riener Publishers, 1999). For an account of how international aid sustained Siad Barre's dictatorship in Somalia, see Michael Maren, *The Road to Hell: The Ravaging Effects of Foreign Aid and International Charity* (New York: Free Press, 1997).

12. See Douglass C. North and Robert P. Thomas, "An Economic Theory of the Growth of the Western World," *Economic History Review*, 2nd series, 28 (1970): 1–17, and Douglass C. North, *Institutions, Institutional Change, and Economic Performance* (New York: Cambridge University Press, 1990). On the importance of institutions see Daron Acemoglu and James A. Robinson, *The Colonial Origins of Comparative Development: An Empirical Investigation*, NBER Working Paper 7771, 2000, and Acemoglu and Robinson, *Economic Backwardness in Political Perspective*, NBER Working Paper 8831, 2002. The leading alternative theory of underdevelopment, associated with Jeffrey Sachs, currently concerns the impact of geography on development. See Jeffrey D. Sachs and Andrew Warner, *Natural Resource Abundance and Economic Growth*, NBER Working Paper 5398, 1995, Sachs, *Tropical Underdevelopment*, NBER Working Paper 8119, 2001,

and, for a direct response to the institutionalist findings of Acemoglu and Robinson, Jeffrey D. Sachs and John W. McArthur, *Institutions and Geography: Comment on Acemoglu, Johnson, and Robinson* (2000), NBER Working Paper 8114, 2001. See also Dani Rodrik and Arvind Subramanian, "The Primacy of Institutions (And What This Does and Does Not Mean)," *Finance and Development* 40, no. 2 (2003): 31–34. William R. Easterly and Ross Levine, *Tropics, Germs, and Crops: How Endowments Influence Economic Development,* NBER Working Paper 9106, 2002.

13. Francis Fukuyama and Sanjay Marwah, "Comparing East Asia and Latin America: Dimensions of Development," *Journal of Democracy* 11, no. 4 (2000): 80–94; Fukuyama, *State-Building: Governance and World Order in the Twenty-First Century* (Ithaca: Cornell University Press, 2004).

14. Francis Fukuyama, "'Stateness' First," *Journal of Democracy* 16, no. 1 (2005): 84–88.

15. For a historical overview, see Nils Gilman, *Mandarins of the Future: Modernization Theory in Cold War America* (Baltimore: Johns Hopkins University Press, 2003).

16. For the Left, see, inter alia, Vernon Ruttan, "What Happened to Political Development?" *Economic Development and Cultural Change* 39, no. 2 (1991): 265–92, Mark Kesselman, "Order or Movement? The Literature of Political Development as Ideology," *World Politics* 26 (1973): 139–54, and Ian Roxborough, "Modernization Theory Revisited: A Review Essay," *Comparative Studies in Society and History* 30 (1988): 753–61. Samuel P. Huntington, *Political Order in Changing Societies* (New Haven: Yale University Press, 1968).

17. See the multivolume work by Philippe C. Schmitter, Guillermo O'Donnell, and Laurence Whitehead, *Transitions from Authoritarian Rule* (Baltimore: Johns Hopkins University Press, 1986). On the applicability of this model to postcommunist states, see Valerie Bunce,

"Should Transitologists Be Grounded?" *Slavic Review* 54, no. 1 (1995): 111–27, and Philippe C. Schmitter and Terry Lynn Karl, "The Conceptual Travels of Transitologists and Consolidologists: How Far to the East Should They Attempt to Go?" *Slavic Review* 53, no. 1 (1994): 172–85.

18. Thomas Carothers, "The End of the Transition Paradigm," *Journal of Democracy* 13, no. 1 (2002): 5–21.

19. Adam Przeworski and Fernando Limongi, *Democracy and Development: Political Institutions and Material Well-Being in the World, 1950–1990* (Cambridge: Cambridge University Press, 2000); Seymour Martin Lipset, "Some Social Requisites of Democracy: Economic Development and Political Legitimacy," *American Political Science Review* 53 (1959): 69–105.

20. The process could be emulative without being adaptive and without producing an overall evolution toward political fitness; the shift toward democracy, in other words, could simply be a fad.

21. Charles Tilly, *Coercion, Capital, and European States, AD 990–1990* (Cambridge: Basil Blackwell, 1990); Douglass North and Arthur Denzu, "Shared Mental Models: Ideologies and Institutions," *Kyklos* 47, no. 1 (1994): 3–31.

22. Ghia Nodia, "Debating the Transition Paradigm: The Democratic Path," *Journal of Democracy* 13, no. 3 (2002): 13–19.

23. This began in many ways with Theda Skocpol and Peter B. Evans, *Bringing the State Back In* (Cambridge: Cambridge University Press, 1985). See also J. P. Nettl, "The State as a Conceptual Variable," *World Politics* 20, no. 4 (1968): 559–92, and Michael Mann, "The Autonomous Power of the State," in John A. Hall, ed., *States in History* (New York: Blackwell, 1986; originally published in *European Journal of Sociology* 25, no. 2 [1984]: 185–213).

24. Thomas Carothers, *Aiding Democracy Abroad: The Learning Curve* (Washington, D.C.: Carnegie Endowment, 1999), and Carothers,

Critical Mission: Essays on Democracy Promotion (Washington, D.C.: Carnegie Endowment, 2004).

25. *President Discusses the Future of Iraq.* With regard to regime change, only Afghanistan among recent cases resembles Germany and Japan in the thoroughness with which it has rejected the political order in place before the U.S. intervention.

26. See the chapter on Bosnia in James Dobbins et al., *America's Role in Nation-Building: From Germany to Iraq* (Santa Monica, Calif.: Rand Corporation, MR-1753-RC, 2003); Gerald Knaus and Felix Martin, "Travails of the European Raj," *Journal of Democracy* 14, no. 3 (2003): 60–74.

27. This was the theme of Jeanne Kirkpatrick, "Dictatorships and Double Standards," *Commentary* 68, no. 11 (November 1979): 34–45. There is continuing controversy over the Nixon administration's role in the coup that brought down the Allende government in Chile.

28. See Thomas Carothers, *In the Name of Democracy: U.S. Policy Toward Latin America in the Reagan Years* (Berkeley: University of California Press, 1993), and Carothers, *Aiding Democracy Abroad: The Learning Curve* (Washington, D.C.: Carnegie Endowment, 1999).

Vice President Cheney once suggested that America's intervention in El Salvador during that country's civil war in the 1980s might be a model for Iraq. But in El Salvador we had a strong democratic ally in the person of President José Napolean Duarte. The U.S. Congress imposed a "light footprint" of no more than fifty-five American military advisers, which meant that the Salvadorians themselves had to bear the brunt of the struggle for their own freedom. The fact that the United States had no organized local allies in Iraq similar to the Salvadorian Christian Democrats or the Northern Alliance in Afghanistan should have been a warning.

29. Eric C. Bjornlund, *Beyond Free and Fair: Monitoring Elections and Building Democracy* (Baltimore: Johns Hopkins University Press, 2004).

30. This is not to say that there are no prodemocracy activists in Russia,

China, or the Arab world but rather that their chances of mobilizing broad antiregime sentiment are lower than in other places.

31. Michael Mandelbaum, "Foreign Policy as Social Work," *Foreign Affairs* 75, no. 1 (1996): 16–32.

32. Fareed Zakaria, *The Future of Freedom: Illiberal Democracy at Home and Abroad* (New York: Norton, 2003).

33. The Millennium Development Goals were adopted at the U.N. Millennium Summit in 2000 and consist of eight broad objectives for improving the condition of poor countries by the year 2015. See Jeffrey D. Sachs, *The End of Poverty: Economic Possibilities for Our Time* (New York: Penguin Press, 2005). Carol Adelman argues that private voluntary giving amounts to $35 billion a year, or 3.5 times as much as official ODA. She counts private remittances in this figure, however, which inflates it tremendously beyond the official USAID estimate of $15 billion in private aid. (By this logic, Mexican and Philippino guestworkers in the United States sending money home to their families, as well as American parents paying tuition for their children to go to Oxford, would count as individuals providing private overseas development assistance.) Carol Adelman, "The Privatization of Foreign Aid: Reassessing National Largesse," *Foreign Affairs* 82, no. 6 (2003): 9–14.

34. See Michael A. Clemens, Charles J. Kenny, and Todd J. Moss, "The Trouble with the MDGs: Confronting Expectations of Aid and Development Success" (Washington: Center for Global Development Working Paper No. 40, May 1, 2004).

35. For an overview, see Steven Radelet, *Challenging Foreign Aid: A Policymaker's Guide to the Millennium Challenge Account* (Washington, D.C.: Center for Global Development, 2003). See also Radelet, "Bush and Foreign Aid," *Foreign Affairs* 82, no.5 (2003): 104–17.

36. Joseph S. Nye, Jr., *Soft Power: The Means to Success in World Politics* (New York: Public Affairs, 2004).

37. For an early history of USAID, see Judith Tendler, *Inside Foreign Aid* (Baltimore: Johns Hopkins University Press, 1975).

38. Jeremy M. Weinstein, John E. Porter, and Stuart Eisenstadt, eds., *On the Brink: Weak States and U.S. National Security* (Washington, D.C.: Center for Global Development, 2004).

39. Redistributing USAID's functions in this fashion would orphan a number of the agency's activities, like the military assistance program (EMET) and funds that have overtly political purposes in support of U.S. foreign policy, such as assistance to Egypt and Israel. These types of programs, which do not even pretend to have a humanitarian or developmental purpose, should properly remain with the State Department. Breaking them off from the general foreign assistance budget would, moreover, give Americans a better idea of how many taxpayer dollars are actually going to support developing countries.

Chapter 6. Rethinking Institutions for World Order

1. For a comprehensive discussion of the legitimacy of U.N. action, see the new foreword to the paperback edition of Robert Kagan, *Of Paradise and Power: America vs. Europe in the New World Order* (New York: Knopf, 2004), and Kagan, "America's Crisis of Legitimacy," *Foreign Affairs* 83, no. 2 (2004): 65–87.

2. See Daniel P. Moynihan, "The United States in Opposition," *Commentary* 59, no. 3 (1975): 31–45.

3. See James Dobbins et al., *The UN's Role in Nation-Building: From the Congo to Iraq* (Santa Monica, Calif.: Rand Corporation, MG-304-RC, 2005); Richard K. Betts, "The Delusion of Impartial Intervention," *Foreign Affairs* 73, no. 6 (1994): 20–33.

4. For an overview, see Virginia Haufler, *International Business Self-Regulation: The Intersection of Public and Private Interests* (Washington, D.C.: Carnegie Endowment for International Peace, 1999), and Haufler, *A Public Role for the Private Sector: Industry Self-Regulation in*

a Global Economy (Washington, D.C.: Carnegie Endowment for International Peace, 2001). There is by now a large literature on NGOs as international actors; see Jessica Tuchman Mathews, "Power Shift," *Foreign Affairs* 76, no. 1 (1997): 50–66, and Ann M. Florini, *The Third Force: The Rise of Transnational Civil Society* (Washington, D.C.: Carnegie Endowment, 2000). On soft law see Kenneth W. Abbott and Duncan Snidal, "Hard and Soft Law in International Governance," *International Organization* 54, no. 3 (2000): 421–56.

5. For a critique of NGO participation in international agreements, see Daniel C. Thomas, "International NGOs, State Sovereignty, and Democratic Values," *Chicago Journal of International Law* 2, no. 2 (2001): 389–97.

6. Naomi Roht-Arriaza, "Shifting the Point of Regulation: The International Organization for Standardization and Global Law," *Ecology Law Quarterly* 22 (1995): 479–539.

7. Anne-Marie Slaughter, *A New World Order* (Princeton: Princeton University Press, 2004).

8. John R. Bolton, "Should We Take Global Governance Seriously?" *Chicago Journal of International Law* 1, no. 2 (2000): 205–21; Jeremy Rabkin, *Why Sovereignty Matters* (Washington, D.C.: American Enterprise Institute, 1998); Rabkin, *The Case for Sovereignty: Why the World Should Welcome American Independence* (Washington, D.C.: AEI Press, 2004).

9. Roht-Arriaza, "Shifting the Point of Regulation"; Marsha Echols, "Food Safety Regulation in the EU and the U.S.: Different Cultures, Different Laws," *Columbia Journal of European Law* 23 (1998): 525–43; Ved Nanda, "Genetically Modified Food and International Law— The Biosafety Protocol and Regulations in Europe," *Denver Journal of International Law and Policy* 28, no. 3 (2000): 235–63; and Robert Paarlberg, "The Global Food Fight," *Foreign Affairs* 79, no. 3 (2000): 24–38.

10. Zoe Baird, "Governing the Internet," *Foreign Affairs* 81, no. 6 (2002): 15–21; Milton Mueller, "ICANN and Internet Governance: Sorting Through the Debris of 'Self-Regulation,'" *Info* 1, no. 6 (1999): 5–8; David R. Johnson and Susan P. Crawford, "Why Consensus Matters: The Theory Underlying ICANN's Mandate to Set Policy Standards for the Domain Name System," *ICANN Watch*, 2000, at www.icannwatch.org/archive/why_consensus_matters.htm.

11. William J. Drake, "The Rise and Decline of the International Telecommunications Regime," in Christopher T. Marsden, *Regulating the Global Information Society* (London: Routledge, 2000). ICANN's functions were performed in the early days of the Internet by a single ponytailed, sandal-wearing graduate student named Jon Postel, who worked at the University of Southern California under contract to the Defense Advanced Projects Agency.

12. Michael A. Froomkin, "Wrong Turn in Cyberspace: Using ICANN to Route Around the APA and the Constitution," *Duke Law Journal* 50, no. 17 (2000): 17–184.

13. For a fuller elaboration of this proposal, see Francis Fukuyama, "Re-Envisioning Asia," *Foreign Affairs* 84, no. 1 (2005): 75–87.

14. Rabkin, *Case for Sovereignty*.

15. Stephen D. Krasner, *Sovereignty: Organized Hypocrisy* (Princeton: Princeton University Press, 1999).

16. Stephen D. Krasner, "Sharing Sovereignty: New Institutions for Collapsed and Failing States," *International Security* 29, no. 2 (2004): 85–120.

Chapter 7: A Different Kind of American Foreign Policy

1. See, for example, Robert W. Merry, *Sands of Empire: Missionary Zeal, American Foreign Policy, and the Hazards of Global Ambition* (New York: Simon and Schuster, 2005), and David Rief, *At the Point of a Gun: Democratic Dreams and Armed Interventions* (New York: Simon and Schuster, 2005).

2. What I have labeled realistic Wilsonianism could be alternatively described as a hard-headed liberal internationalism. This is distinguished from the soft-headed version by several characteristics: first, the United States should work toward a multi-multilateral world, not give special emphasis to the United Nations; second, the goal of foreign policy is not the transcendence of sovereignty and power politics but its regularization through institutional constraints; and finally, democratic legitimacy embedded in real institutions ought to guide the design of the system overall.

3. See "President Bush Discusses Freedom in Iraq and the Middle East: Remarks by the President at the 20th Anniversary of the National Endowment for Democracy," Washington, D.C., Nov. 6, 2003. In her interview in *The American Interest*, Rice states, "When it comes to the question of whether you might, in fact, get extremists elected . . . I think you have to ask yourself if you are better off in a situation where extremists, Islamists and others, get to hide behind their masks and operate on the fringes of the political system, or would you rather have an open political system in which people have to actually contest for the will of the people?"

4. It might be possible to argue for an authoritarian transition in the Middle East if one could find any truly modernizing autocrats in the region, comparable to Park Chung-Hee of South Korea or Lee Kuan Yew of Singapore. The vast majority of Arab autocrats have shown little interest in development and have been very clever in preventing democratic openings from proceeding beyond a few initial small steps. See Daniel Brumberg, "Liberalization Versus Democracy," in Thomas Carothers and Marina Ottaway, eds., *Uncharted Journey: Promoting Democracy in the Middle East* (Washington, D.C.: Carnegie Endowment, 2005).

5. An example of the former is Europe's refusal to go along with an American effort to have Mohamed El-Baradei removed as head of the International Atomic Energy Agency; an example of the latter is the stead-

fast refusal of France and Germany to participate in the reconstruction of Iraq.

6. G. John Ikenberry, *After Victory: Institutions, Strategic Restraint, and the Rebuilding of Order After Major Wars* (Princeton: Princeton University Press, 2001).

7. Zbigniew Brzezinski, "The Dilemma of the Last Sovereign," *American Interest* 1, no. 1 (2005): 37–46.

8. Pierre Hassner, "Definitions, Doctrines, and Divergences," *National Interest* no. 69 (2002): 30–34.

Index

Index

Index

Murray, Charles, 18–19, 20
Muslims, 69–70; cultural diversity of, 75. *See also* jihadists
mutual assured destruction (MAD), 33
Myroie, Laurie, 203n21

Nasser, Gamal Abdel, 85
National Democratic Institute (NDI), 150
National Endowment for Democracy (NED), 134, 137, 150, 187
national greatness, 42–43
National Interest, 20, 40
National Security Strategy of the United States (NSS), 3, 81–83, 88, 101, 104, 142, 184, 201–2n11
nation-building, 9–10, 63–64, 131, 151–52; George W. Bush's views on, 46; and democracy promotion, 125; in North and South Vietnam, 121; United Nation's role in, 161. *See also* democratic transitions
NATO (North Atlantic Treaty Organization), 52, 64, 99, 176; and Iraq war, 174; legitimacy of, 172–74; as security organization, 172; U.S. relationship with, 173–74
natural right, 23
neoclassical economics, 44, 199n26
neoconservatism: as approach to U.S. foreign policy, 7–8, 46–47; attacks on, 13, 183; and communism, 50–51; and the Kristol-Kagan agenda, 40–44; roots of, 14–21; Strauss as influence on, 13, 21–31; and traditional conservatism, 38–39, 44–45; underlying principles of, 4–5, 9, 13–14, 48–49; Wohlstetter as influence on, 31–36
neoconservatives: and Bush administration foreign policy, 3–4, 12–14,

61–65; debate among, regarding foreign policy, 39–40; during the Cold War, 59–60, 62–63; and international institutions, 49, 64–65; and preventive-war doctrine, 102–3; threat as perceived by, 62
New Left, 18
Nicaragua, 135
Nietzsche, Friedrich, 24
Nitze, Paul, 38, 50
Niyazov, Saparmurat, 130
nonbinding agreements, 165
Nonproliferation Treaty (NPT), 32
North, Douglass, 122, 129–30
North Atlantic Treaty Organization. *See* NATO
North Korea, 80, 91, 174–75
Norton, Anne, 21
nuclear deterrence, 32–33, 68
nuclear proliferation, 32–33; in the Middle East, 34, 80–81
Nye, Joseph, 149

Office of Democracy, Human Rights, and Labor (DRL), 150
Oil for Food scandal, 65, 80, 96
Olsen, Mancur, 99–100
Open Society Institute, 137
Orange Revolution, 136
Organisation for Economic Co-operation and Development (OECD), 142–43
Organization for Security and Cooperation in Europe (OSCE), 175, 176
Osirak reactor, 85, 90
Otpor, 137
overseas development assistance (ODA), 142–43, 147

Pakistan, 91; economic development in, 119; as nuclear power, 80, 88

Index

Palestine: as issue in the Arab world, 76–77
Parsons, Talcott, 126
Patriot Act, 1
Perle, Richard, 12, 31, 51
Personal Responsibility and Work Opportunity Reconciliation Act (1996), 20
Philippines, 132, 135
Pillar, Paul, 68
Pinochet, Augusto, 135
Plato, 25, 30
Podhoretz, Norman, 14, 17
Poland, 29, 136
political development, 125–31, 140, 185; and competition, 129–30; and democratic transitions, 127–28, 140; and economic development, 128–29; ideas as basis for, 130
Pollack, Kenneth, 89
Popper, Karl, 24
Portugal, 133–34
Postel, Jon, 214n11
poverty: Moynihan's views on, 20. *See also* economic development
Powell, Colin, 61, 92, 100, 106, 183
preemptive action, doctrine of, 1–2, 62, 81–83, 104; as distinguished from preventive war, 84–88; justification for, 2–3, 6
Presidential Decision Directive, 56, 151–52
preventive-war doctrine, 6, 62; as Bush administration policy, 82–83, 92–94, 101, 183, 190, 202n11; criteria for, 104–5, 184; as distinguished from preemptive action, 84–88; problems inherent in, 85–86, 90–91, 93–94, 178
Protestant Reformation, 77–78
Przeworksi, Adam, 128
public health in developing countries, 120, 143

Public Interest, 17–21, 38, 115
Putin, Vladimir, 58
Pye, Lucian, 126

al-Qaida, 1, 62, 105; and ties to Iraq, 79, 89
Qutb, Sayyid, 73

Rabkin, Jeremy, 167, 177
radio broadcasts, 136, 150
Radio Farda, 150
Radio Free Europe/Radio Liberty, 136, 150
Radio SAWA, 150
Reagan Ronald, 34, 38, 52, 199n27; as neoconservative, 45–46; and the Soviet Union, 46, 50–51, 57, 59
realistic Wilsonianism, 9–10, 184, 215n2
realists (in foreign policy), 7, 8, 9, 61, 114, 157, 183; neoconservative opposition to, 37
reason and political order, 30
reform: in the Arab world, 187; as stimulated by financial incentives, 145–46, 178
regime: idea of, 25–26, 29–30, 48; role of politics in, 26–27, 48
regime change, 133–38; as advocated by Kristol and Kagan, 41–42, 56; as aspect of Bush administration policy, 8, 28–31, 36, 55, 63–64, 91, 178, 182; in Eastern Europe, 51–53, 136–38. *See also* democratic transitions
Republican Party, and foreign policy issues, 43
Rice, Condoleezza, 46, 104, 183, 186, 215n3
Roosevelt, Franklin, 45
Roosevelt, Theodore, 42
Rose Revolution, 136
Rostow, Walt, 121, 126

Index

Roy, Olivier, 71–72, 77, 186, 201n5
Rubin, Barry, 76
Rubin, Robert, 109, 110
Rumsfeld, Donald, 4, 36, 63–64, 98–99, 181, 183
Russert, Tim, 115
Rycroft, Matthew, 195n1

Sachs, Jeffrey, 142, 144, 207n12
Salazar, António de Oleveira, 133
SALT (Strategic Arms Limitations Talks) treaty, 34
Saudi Arabia, American presence in, 79
Scowcroft, Brent, 8
Security Council (U.N.), 2–3, 92, 96–97, 100; effectiveness of, 161–62; legitimacy of, 161; and security threats, 160, 161
security policy: assumptions underlying, 67–68; role of international institutions in, 172, 174–75
Selznick, Philip, 15
September 11, 2001, attacks: Bush administration's response to, 1–2, 190; European response to, 68–69; threat assessment following, 5–6, 66–69, 78, 92, 200n1
Serbia, 98, 136, 137
Sestanovich, Stephen, 99
Shils, Edward, 126
Slaughter, Anne-Marie, 166
social engineering: as aspect of rebuilding of Iraq, 6–7, 9; during the 1960s, 18; limits of, 19, 114–16; neoconservative view of, 5, 49, 62
Socrates, 25, 28–29, 30
soft law, 165
soft-power institutions, 149–54, 185
Solidarity labor union, 136
Soros, George, 137
South Korea, 135, 174–75

sovereignty, 9; European view of, 159; and global order, 157, 177–79; shared, 179–80
Soviet Union, 199–200n32; collapse of, 52–53, 59; détente with, 37–38; as nuclear threat, 33–34
Stalin, Joseph, 16
START (Strategic Arms Reduction Talks) Treaty, 165
State Department, U.S. See foreign policy, U.S.; U.S. Agency for International Development
states: horizontal accountability among, 156; legitimacy of, 10; as shaper of outcomes, 130–31. See also nation-building; sovereignty
strategic arms control, 34
Strauss, Leo, 13, 21–31, 193, 197n9; and idea of "regime," 25, 26–27, 29–30, 31; as philosopher, 22, 23; political views of, 22–23; politicization of ideas of, 23
Strauss-Kahn, Dominique, 100
structural adjustment loans, 109, 121–22, 145–47
Students for a Democratic Society, 18
Summers, Larry, 109

Taliban regime, 1
targeting precision, 35
techno-libertarianism, 108–9, 205n12
technology, American, 107–8, 205n13
Tennessee Valley Authority, 119
terrorism: background conditions facilitating, 142; as threat to Europe, 185, 186. See also jihadists; September 11, 2001, attacks
Thernstrom, Abigail, 18–19
Thernstrom, Stephan, 18–19
Third Wave of democratization, 57, 127, 131
Thucydides, 192

After the Neocons